Also by Gail Wilson Kenna

Story of a Contrary, Contumacious Cat
Here to There and Back Again
Beyond the Wall
A Soul-Making Keats Collection

Tennis Talk of a Nobody

Gail Wilson Kenna

Crosshill Creek Publications

Tennis Talk of a Nobody

Printed in the United States of America
Crosshill Creek Publications
P.O. Box 216, Wicomico Church, VA 22579

A. Cort Sinnes, design
Hearth & Garden Productions

Library of Congress Control Number: Pending
Kenna, Gail Wilson *Tennis Talk of a Nobody*

ISBN 978-1-7341602-5-3

Dedicated to my father, Robert Theron Wilson, to Dr. Robert Coles, my literary hero, to Dr. William E. Nordt, the finest of orthopedic surgeons, and to my enduring husband, Mike

DOUBLE WINNER — Gail Wilson looms as favorite to cop both the Girls 18-and-under and Girls 15-and-under division of the Fullerton City Junior Tennis Tournament. She plays winner of the Judy Anderson-Glenda Gray match tonight at 5:30. Wilson is ranked among the top ten amongst Southern California junior girls of her age group.   (News Tribune Photo)

Table of Contents

My father, Robert Wilson, at USC in the late 1920s.

The Warm-Up

Talking about tennis is my way to toss a box with a large collection of yellowed newspaper articles and clippings. This box has traveled with me to twenty-four apartments & houses, seventeen cities, and five other countries. In all these many moves, countless things were donated and discarded. Not the box.

The other day I again heard a common lament about the proliferation and publication of memoirs. Confession, recollection, and reminiscence were words used. The speaker compared the genre of memoir to a pool by the sea, which as the tide recedes, reveals our vain obsession with self. This is why I decided to begin this book with Emily Dickinson's short poem, *I'm nobody. Who are you?*

> I'm a Nobody! Who are you?
> Are you – Nobody – Too?
> Then there's a pair of us!
> Don't tell! they'd advertise – you know!
>
> How dreary – to be – Somebody!
> How public – like a Frog –
> To tell one's name – the livelong June –
> To an admiring Bog!

Yet something in me must also include a quote from *The Mind's Fate* by Dr. Robert Coles. "The mind's fate is, after all, a person's fate. We are drawn along our private visions, but beyond them stretch almost infinitely to each of us the vast and compelling mysteries of Chance and Circumstance."

I capitalized two nouns in the quote for a reason. *Tennis Talk of a Nobody* is a weave of narratives within a frame, and if the strings were cut from my tennis racquet, everything in life changes. Without tennis I would not be a writer. Back in 1975, I enrolled in writing courses at U.C. Berkeley after the experience I recount in "The Summer of Watergate." And were it not for the epistolary tradition, I would not have written my first book, which is a fictionalized account of my great-great-grandfather's 1849 Gold Rush letters. Through this and other experiences, I came to see memories as letters received from the past, often written with invisible ink, which require a special concentrated light to understand what they tell us about experience. And to understand experience requires reflection and language.

The narratives in this book cover seven decades of tennis, the sport in and out of my life. The writings are episodic, not chronological, and written over the past few years. I hope my reader sees this collection as larger than one tennis player and the mysteries of chance and circumstance in her life. Lastly, *Tennis Talk of a Nobody* honors my father, Robert Theron Wilson, whose desire that his daughter play competitive tennis, gave me the life I have led, and for which I feel the deepest gratitude.

Obituaries . . .

ROBERT T. WILSON, 79

Memorial services will be held Sunday for Robert Theron Wilson, 79, who died June 10 in Palomar Hospital. His home was in Pauma Valley where he had lived for the past 14 years.

A native of Arkansas, he lived most of his life in Fullerton. He was a graduate of the University of Southern California and a long-time employee of Sunkist Growers.

For many years he managed the harbor operations of that organization. Since his retirement had been an avocado grower and Calavo member.

Survivors include his wife, Barbara, a son, Barry of Yorba Linda, daughter, Gail of Washington, D.C., a brother, Byron of Fullerton; and four grandchildren.

Memorial services will be held at 4 p.m. Sunday at Pauma Valley Community Church. The family requests contributions be made to the American Heart Assn. or Children's Home Society, Casa de Cuna Auxiliary.

Above: *With my father, Fullerton, California, 1944.*

11

Set One

The Weave of Tennis

During the 1950s, a single strand of cat gut was strung through a wood racquet. Only when a string broke was there awareness of the tight weave giving way. Gut frayed, which made it possible to see how close a string was to breaking. Not so with today's synthetic strings. Until one snaps there's little forewarning. Cut tennis strings from my life and so much disappears. Now at 79, I dread the day when I'll be unable to play a sport that has characterized my life.

Ironically, tennis was not my first choice. More than anything, I had wanted to play the piano. My family didn't have one. Grandmother Wilson did, and on this upright piano, her adult younger son played popular tunes from earlier decades. Between the second and fifth grades, I often sat beside my uncle while he played sheet music I had selected earlier from inside the piano bench. Byron was something of a Boo Radley character, unable to cope with adults other than Grandmother, with whom he lived on Rose Drive in Fullerton, California. I never thought of my uncle as odd until pubescence. And earlier he had fed my fantasies of playing the piano. Father had another idea. My older brother, a swimmer, a bit slow on pigeon-toed feet, was not destined to be the tennis champ that Father hoped to have.

My first tennis lesson in fifth grade left me in tears. I disliked John, an arrogant man unlike Tanny in Los Angeles, the pro who years later gave me polished strokes. From my first lesson with this Romanian & European champion, I welcomed his tan arms around me, a teacher who demonstrated strokes through touch, feel, and few words. In contrast, I did not like John's hairy, sweaty arms around me. In my first lesson I swung as if hitting a softball, stiff like a bat. Father was there and his face showed disappointment. But John, after talking to my father, and not charging for the first lesson, sent me home to practice a forehand swing in front of a full-length mirror. I did this religiously until my second lesson.

In 1953 my family did not have the money for multiple lessons. Grandmother Wilson had promised to buy a piano if Father paid for a teacher. This was not to be. A dreamy child, who preferred hours with books and dolls, who liked to skate alone and wander the seashore at Newport Beach two weeks each June, found herself in a world where the external mattered and inner voices had to be silenced.

In summer 2011 at the Bread Loaf Writers' Conference, my instructor, Luis Urrea, asked his class to write a six-word memoir. I wrote several but ended up reading aloud the one on tennis: *My broken foot, Billie Jean's look.* Ms. King went on to fame, a tennis stadium in New York named after her. She attended L.A. State when I was at the University of Southern California, and sometimes our tennis teams practiced together. Billie Jean had a Wimbledon doubles title by then. During a 1963 college tournament in Tucson, Arizona, the two of us were housed together in a sorority. Over breakfast one morning, I noted again how Billie Jean had made tennis her concentration in life. To achieve success in the sport demanded a singular focus. Years earlier at a La Jolla junior tournament, she had told a group of us that one day she would be the best female tennis player in the world. She encouraged us to get up and practice volleys on the lawn. Or to dash out to empty courts as she did, and practice serves until players arrived for a match. Sipping cokes and watching boys had more attraction. But I sensed then that Billie Jean's determination and natural gifts meant she would realize her dream.

What does this have to do with my six-word memoir? The time was June 1960 in Burlingame, Northern California, at the National Junior Hardcourt championships. This tournament was the first stop on the Pacific Northwest tour, which I was to play that summer. The tour would end in Canada on grass courts in Victoria and Vancouver. I'd earned money for this by working after school during my junior year of high school. Gerald Boege, the owner of the local sporting goods store, believed in youth tennis and helped young players. My tennis partner, Mary Jo, and I became the secretary at Boege and Bean. That school year I worked Monday through Thursday, and Mary Jo handled Friday afternoons and Saturday mornings. Our intent was to save enough money for the tour. If my tennis had not slipped the year before, I might have been going East that summer of 1960, on a tour that ended in Forest Hills at the U.S. National Championships. That was where Billie Jean headed after Burlingame. Yet I held to a hope that by winning tournaments in Oregon, Washington, Canada, and playing on both clay and grass, that I might work my way back and be ranked high enough to go East the following summer.

The afternoon of my first match in Burlingame, I fell on a single court, the only one I had ever seen. No alleys for doubles. I remember wanting to ask for another court, feeling disoriented at one so shrunken. Toward the end of the match, winning easily, I ran for a short shot close to the net, stopped too quickly, twisted to the left, fell backward, and broke all five metatarsal bones in my left foot. I only learned this medical fact later. Dr. Palmer, the father of the famous Palmer tennis-playing-family from Arizona, came out on the court and said I should stop immediately. I didn't. I won the match and went to a dance that night, convinced that whatever was wrong with my foot would be gone in the morning so I could play my next match, as well as doubles with Mary Jo.

By midnight I was in the emergency room of the local hospital.

When I fell that day, I'd glanced into the bleachers and seen Billie Jean's face. Mary Jo lost to her several days later in the tournament semi-finals. I wasn't there. I'd taken a train home to Southern California, carrying my new set of matching racquets and one suitcase, wondering if Father would be alive when I reached Los Angeles.

At the same hour when I broke my foot (and I'd never fallen on a court in seven years of play), Father began vomiting blood in a strawberry field near Newport Beach. There was no phone at the beach house, which my parents rented to tenants all year except for the first two weeks in June when they took their vacations. I sent a telegram there. "Broken foot. Coming home."

16

Somehow, a neighbor at the beach intercepted the telegram and contacted my mother in Fullerton. She reached me through the tournament committee in Burlingame. I learned what had happened and was told that if Mother's friend Dorothy Lakeman was at the L.A. train station to meet me, then Father had died during a surgery to save his life. If my brother Barry was at the station, Father had survived the removal of half his stomach. I remember thinking on the train that if Dorothy were there, I would not have to bear again my father's disappointment that I'd failed at tennis.

Looking back to 1960, it is strange that I should have been housed in Burlingame at the home of two physicians. I remember how she (whose name I have forgotten) expressed surprise that I hadn't broken down in tears at the hospital when she and her husband told me that five broken metatarsal bones meant I would not be playing tennis for quite some time. Only I understood the stoic mask the physicians saw that night. The accident provided an excuse to hang up my racquets. There was Mother's relief, too. With a full-time job, how could she care for her husband? I became Father's nurse that summer after his recovery from near death in a strawberry field.

In Burlingame I'd been given a temporary cast, so in Fullerton my foot had to be reset. After the cast was cut off, I sat on a cold metal table. The orthopedic, using the instrument in his hand, tapped below each knee. Nothing. No reaction in either leg. I was sent to the lab for blood tests. The results showed I had a malfunctioning thyroid. This medical fact ought to have vindicated me for the decline in my tennis at sixteen, when I was a top ten player in Southern California. No wonder I had gained weight, no longer ran quickly, lugged an enervated body around tennis courts and hallways at school. Most of all during my sophomore year, I had wanted to sleep in my dark room at home. It is not easy to revisit memories of those days and my deep sense of failure.

Yesterday my USC Alumni magazine arrived. The sketch of a cello caught my eye. The inaugural Piatigorsky International Cello Festival had just taken place at the USC Thornton School of Music. Why do I mention this? Several times I went with my tennis coach to Gregor Piatigorsky's court in Beverly Hills. His son was one of Tanny's pupils. I haven't forgotten my first time there and the sounds of a cello from a music studio near the tennis court. I learned the man playing was recognized throughout the world. While picking up balls for Tanny, I listened to this famous cellist. Oh, to play a musical instrument! But if tennis began as compensation for not playing the piano, tennis revealed a world beyond Orange County, California.

I recall the day when I played doubles with Tanny against a man and a frail-looking woman with fading red hair. Only after we finished did I learn who the woman was: Helen Wills Moody, a famous female tennis player. Another day when Mother came to pick me up at Will Rogers State Park in Los Angeles where Tanny taught, she could not believe her eyes. I was hitting balls to Walter Pigeon, a movie star she idolized. There was the night I went to a party at Monica Henreid's house and met her father, a movie star named Paul. *Casablanca*, for god's sake! When my friends were drooling over Ricky Nelson on the weekly television show, *Ozzie and Harriet*, I was chatting with him at tournaments. I recall the night at a tournament in Bakersfield when Ricky Nelson began singing an Elvis Presley song and told a group of us that he was going to be a rock and roll star. What a sad end. A burning plane and flames engulfing fame.

Besides the L.A. world of movie stars, I met famous players and thought little of it. Pancho Seguro and Pancho Gonzalez gave clinics, as did Maureen (Little Mo) Connolly in San Diego one time. Once at a tournament I stayed in a house that belonged to Jack Kramer's parents. Another time Rod Laver stood behind a court and watched me play a match at the L.A. tennis club during the Pacific Southwest, a tournament that followed the U.S. National Championships and attracted top men and women players. After my match, Rod Laver told me I had a terrific forehand and teased that my hair was redder than his. Tennis was a small world then, and Australia was the country that produced top players, along with the United States. To be a top player in Southern California meant being among the best players everywhere.

The tennis world then and now could be separate galaxies.

This morning, looking at the marshlands of Mill Creek in the Northern Neck of Virginia, I have told myself to write like the wind whistling outside my study. To be in other words, a gale with words. The strong wind reminded me of late winter and early spring tournaments in Southern California. I would win because privileged girls from Los Angeles did not play well when the wind blew. They were accustomed to courts with wind breaks at their oasis of the Los Angeles Tennis Club. If today I were to meet Billie Jean King, I would want to discuss the discrimination that she and I faced when we were young. That is until she became too good to be ignored. Though later this tennis champion would face discrimination related to her gender and sexuality.

Through tennis I learned about unfairness. Not just the obvious cheating that occurred on the court. I speak of the behind-the-scenes variety; that someone like me who outranked girls from the L.A. Tennis club would be excluded from special competitions there while lower ranked girls were invited. The sport, after all, was associated with wealth and private clubs, despite Althea Gibson and the two Panchos, who beat the odds to become champions. During the early 1950s, small communities like Fullerton started Youth Tennis Foundations. That was when some local men hired John as a tennis instructor. Yet the only place he had to teach was the local high school with its ten cement courts, which were nothing more than big slabs of concrete, cracks and all, and wire nets.

I haven't forgotten the first time I played on a sunken court in Los Angeles at a prestigious country club. The solitary court below ground level was protected from the wind. The sound of the ball literally blew me away, as did its speed. Cement was slow. The dark gray hardcourt was smooth like glass, with balls flying off it. That day I played a private school girl named Ann. She wore a pink cardigan sweater with her school's crest. To pick up a ball she tapped it with her racquet. I tried to copy her. But my racquet smashed against the court, the ball not budging. That day I beat Ann, who was all polish and no guts. When I met

Tanny and became his pupil, I was all guts and no polish. Then I was guts and polish, then fearful and polished, and eventually only fearful of losing, of disappointing Father and Tanny. The conflict in me was a chasm into which I fell when I walked on a court at a tournament. I wasn't fearful of someone better, even welcomed a seventeen-year-old ranked player. No, my fall began when I saw my name as the first seed in fifteen-and-under. I especially felt fear if my next opponent was a known dinker, which meant a player who pushed balls relentlessly. I had a strong forehand and backhand, but my forehand broke down when an opponent soft-balled shots.

The summer before my sophomore year, I was seeded first in three tournaments and lost in the quarter-finals of each. I had trouble concentrating, had put on weight, wanted to take long naps, often fell asleep in class. My grades of A's from freshman year slipped to a smattering of lower grades, even a C in geometry. I took to wearing heavy coats to school, dropped my old popular friends, had a recurring dream in which I was in a tunnel, my name being called. Always the same mysterious message: *return to the source*. We'd moved after my freshman year from a rented house to one my parents bought. My new room had no access to the outside. Once my room had been the back of the house, until a prior owner added on a family room, bedroom, second bath, and garage. My room had two large windows, one on each side of its back wall. The windows were heavily draped and hid the family room. There was not a ceiling light in my bedroom, only a small lamp on the desk and another above my bed. The recurring dream frightened me, so I began leaving my desk light on. My parents had taken to sleeping in separate bedrooms: my father ill from his frequent travels to Europe for Sunkist Growers. Mother's room was close to mine. She could see through my shuttered doors and would turn off the desk lamp. I would awaken in the dark, unable to utter a sound, as if I were being strangled. Something terrible is happening to me, I must have wanted to say to someone. Instead, I heard a repeated question. *What has happened to your tennis?* Other than Father asking this, people in town looked at me with disappointment. My picture had been in the local newspaper often, with articles about each tournament I played. I had been the darling of the local sports writer. Then I wasn't his favorite, and he began writing about another disappointing loss from Miss Wilson. Even worse, Mother kept at me about my weight. No one spoke of depression in a public way then. My entire sophomore year is one long sweep of darkness, during which I walked with my head down. I don't know if the ill-functioning thyroid caused the depression. Or was it vice versa? I do know it was unusual to be put immediately on the maximum dose of synthetic thyroid, as I was that June of 1960.

Sad as this might sound, my father showed sagacity in wanting me to play tennis. "What are your chances of being great at the piano?" If those weren't his words, they convey my father's hope. Well, I wasn't great at tennis and failed to fulfill his dream of becoming another Little Mo. Yet without the meaningful connections this sport has given me, to cut tennis strings from my life would leave an almost empty frame.

Tennis allowed me to be independent, even if conjoined

to someone else's dream. I see a young girl traveling alone on buses to tournaments in Southern California. From the age of twelve onward, I stayed during tournaments in other people's houses. Some families were delightful, others less so. I smile now, remembering the time in La Jolla when I stayed in a huge, decaying house on a hill above the Pacific Ocean. I met only the husband, never the wife, and was given the bedroom of a boy away at camp. But his snakes were there, coiled in glass cages all around a room with its distasteful smell of reptiles. I'm not sure I slept that week. Yet from experiences like this, I learned to handle odd situations.

During the first year I played tennis, I faced a moral dilemma. Another girl and I were tagged as the two players with potential in Fullerton. Pat Smith attended the Catholic school and was recognized as a gifted softball player. We often practiced together on the high school courts. One afternoon on the white concrete, I wanted to beat Pat so much that I called a ball out on the baseline. It had to have been obvious to Pat that her ball was in. A little voice whispered that I had crossed a moral divide and not to do it again. Cheating was endemic in tennis. The top players then and now are forced to be fair because of referees and linesmen/women, and fancy modern equipment that measures where the ball lands. If I've made wrong calls, they have not been intentional—not after the afternoon with Pat Smith when I was eleven.

Something else important happened because of tennis. It helped me not to envy people of wealth and kept me from yearning to be among *los ricos*. Early on I had to deal with the fact that my racquet could not be smashed and thrown around.

I wore adhesive tape on the toes of my tennis shoes to make them last longer. Back then a pair of Ked tennis shoes cost eight dollars. My first job at Boege and Bean Sporting Goods, and later at a department store, paid a dollar an hour. I had to work two hours to buy a can of new tennis balls.

Yet one day at thirteen, I had a bit of luck. There I was, riding my bicycle downtown to get books at Fullerton's public library. Suddenly, a woman opened her car door as I passed by. The impact threw me into the street, a car swerving to miss me and my bike. (A city ordinance disallowed bikes on sidewalks.)

TENNIS CHAMPIONS — Shown above are se veral of Fullerton's fine tennis players, who Sa day, were presented trophies for winning the rece ntly-concluded Amerige Park net tourney. row, l to r—Gail Wilson, and Mike Hall. Back ro w—Ann Gruther, Sheldon Boege, Pat S Marshall and David Smitt. The players have been taking lessons from Herm Anderson the summer. (News Tri

My knees and right elbow were bloodied, my face (no doubt) red with embarrassment. The elderly woman looked mortified and thrust a piece of paper into my hand with her name, telephone number, and insurance company. I was to play a tournament that weekend but had to withdraw because of my injured elbow. My father called Rodd, my dapper uncle with a law practice in Beverly Hills. The next thing I knew I received a check for one thousand dollars from the woman's insurance company. That was a lot of money then and it became my tennis fund. I had my own bank account, wrote checks for tournament entry fees, paid for lessons, bought my shoes and racquets. The money lasted several years but ran out before the Pacific Northwest. I knew the only way I could go on the tour was to earn the money myself, and I did.

Throughout my life, tennis provided employment: summers during college when I taught for the Fullerton Recreation Department, my starving years in San Francisco during graduate school when I taught for the Youth Tennis Foundation at Golden Gate Park, later the months I taught tennis at Randolph AFB in Texas when my new husband, a student-pilot, earned so little money. I wouldn't have met Mike if I hadn't been a tennis instructor at a posh girl's camp the summer of 1967. I would not be seated where I am now, looking into Mill Creek, were it not for tennis. Everything in my life is connected one way or another to this sport. Cut these strings and everything changes. Now I look back with the deepest gratitude that Father took me to that first lesson with John in Fullerton.

The story is obviously more complicated than these few

pages. And in early morning light, writing on a pad of yellow paper, I stopped to stretch and went downstairs. There, I retrieved a framed photo of my father with his tennis racquet at USC, on the same courts where I practiced decades later. I was on the first tennis team when women were included in the PAC 8 (Pacific Athletic Conference) and we played with the "men" during the end-of-season tournament at Stanford in spring 1964. Our USC coach was instrumental in the establishment of Title 9 sports for women.

I went to USC to please Father, though my family could not afford this private university where he had gone in the 1920s on athletic scholarships. I'd hoped that being a Trojan would mean atonement for giving up the dream of tennis success the summer of 1960. Grafted on, a failure remains. And feelings of failure cannot be cut out like old strings from a tennis frame. I hear Father telling me, "When the going gets tough, the tough get going." I didn't appreciate his words then,

First tennis trophy, age 11. Fullerton, California.

26

though I appreciate them now, in the same way I appreciate his photo from USC, with Father's sleeve rolled like champion Bill Tilden. Robert Theron Wilson would have liked to be a tennis champion and he hoped his only daughter might become one. I have decided to write a book of tennis recollections and dedicate it to my father and hope to better understand through the weave of tennis, the trajectory of my life.

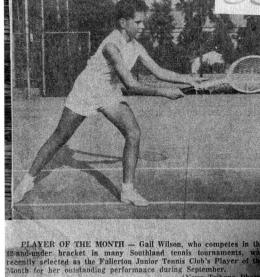

Above: *Second trophy, age 13, but hair cut short — no more braids!*

PLAYER OF THE MONTH — Gail Wilson, who competes in the 12-and-under bracket in many Southland tennis tournaments, was recently selected as the Fullerton Junior Tennis Club's Player of the Month for her outstanding performance during September.
(News Tribune Photo)

Tennis is Why You Exist, Dear Daughters

F irst Carrie Fisher, next Debbie Reynolds—that was the order of the duo getting out of a black limousine in front of the Montecito-Sequoia Lodge that June afternoon in 1967. What struck me was how tiny Reynolds was, and how ridiculous she looked in spike heels, trying to walk on rough mountain terrain. Unlike the star-struck counselors near me, I had seen too many celebrities in the Southern California tennis world to be in awe of Debbie. And for the next four weeks, her daughter made no lasting impression on me, even though Carrie lived in the cabin next to mine. What did impress me was her cabin mate, the daughter of Rod Serling, whose *The Twilight Zone* had been my favorite television series. For a writer like him, I felt awe. A decade later, I saw *Star Wars* at the insistence of two female psychologists in Napa who ran a woman's group, of which I was a member. Carrie Fisher an actress? Who knew? Not I, a decade after that summer job. Now she and her mother have died: Fisher at 60, Reynolds at 84, both deceased within days of each other.

Until now, I have not written about the four weeks that determined my future. How to describe the oddity and improbability of standing among counselors that Sunday afternoon, gawking at a movie star stepping from her dust-layered limo, teetering on high heels in the mountainous terrain of King's Canyon in Central California. The actual road into the camp was dusty and potholed, not unlike my life in 1967.

Five months earlier I had earned my secondary teaching credential from San Francisco State and returned to Southern California to teach for the Los Angeles City Schools. Teaching vacancies in mid-year were limited, so I had to accept a position in a junior high. The school, Dodson, was located near San Pedro. Black and Latino students were bused from there, up to the Pacific Palisades, a white enclave. As the last teacher hired, I was given below-average English classes of seventh and eighth graders. My student teaching had been with sophomores and juniors in high school, which meant I had little idea how to teach junior high English.

At the time the Los Angeles district paid a teacher for ten months of the year. This meant I had no income in July and August. I had debts from graduate school and a monthly car payment. Worst of all, I had lost the love of a doctoral student at UCLA, someone I'd met in 1966 at San Francisco State. In large part I'd moved South because of him. That is another story, though it bears on this one because of Mike Number One's decision to marry someone from his Peace Corps days. His rejection left me bereft. Yet my practical side was not completely frayed. I knew I had to find a summer job away from Los Angeles so I would not have to pay rent for two months. In late May of 1967, I had moved from one apartment in Redondo Beach to another. A former sorority sister had moved out but kept paying rent so her roomies would cover for her. She did not want her parents to know she had moved in with a professor at USC. All of this meant I could stash my things at the apartment and not pay rent until school began. Another sorority sister and good friend lived close by. I asked Annie to help me get a job teaching tennis at a summer camp in Santa Cruz where she had gone as a child and later been a counselor. My old friend felt that I would clash with the owner/director, though she did not tell me this. Ann spoke to the camp director but must not have recommended me. Who knows why, but this camp director passed my name as a potential tennis instructor to Dr. Barnes, a professor at San Jose State, who owned and ran the Montecito-Sequoia camp for girls.

Meanwhile, Mike Kenna had earned his degree at San Jose State (SJS) and had nothing to do until he reported to Air Force pilot training in Texas. He and Jack, his AF-ROTC buddy, answered an advertisement posted at SJS about work at a summer camp for girls. What a lark, they thought. Poor Jack worked his rear off that summer doing manual labor. Mike with his Paul Newman looks was hired to be the rifle instructor.

At some point in late May, Dr. Barnes contacted me and

said to meet her mother at the Biltmore Hotel in downtown Los Angeles. There I met a demure lady, elegantly dressed, with a hat on her white hair. We had tea. The senior Mrs. Barnes had little to say. I was not convinced she was all there. But apparently my appearance and manners passed her inspection. There was a catch, however. The counselors and instructors were to arrive at the camp a week before L.A. schools ended that June. Needing to fill the position, Dr. Barnes waived this requirement for me. This meant I arrived at the camp only one day before Carrie and Debbie stepped from their limo.

Luckily, I missed five days of cleaning the camp, though the dirt in my cabin had been left and the bunks had to be prepared. I remember struggling to get sheets on a top one when two bats flew at me. The room was large enough for three bunk beds and my single bed beside the one window on the back wall. The camp was designed to give rich girls a scouting experience. I had been a Girl Scout and gone to camp several times because it cost little, given we slept on single cots on wood platforms in the open air. No water skiing, sailing instruction, array of stables with horses and ponies, no elaborate rooms for art, music, and theater, and certainly no tennis courts. These activities and others were available at Montecito-Sequoia for a hefty fee.

School for me ended on Friday. I stayed out past midnight with Von, a gorgeous-looking male teacher, a Duke graduate, who is another story. I had been told to be at the camp by late morning, which meant leaving Redondo Beach before 6:00 a.m. These days I experience anxiety about packing for trips and have a recurring dream in which I must get ready for a flight in only minutes. Perhaps the dream is a hangover from that early June morning in 1967. I tossed clothing in a duffle bag, grabbed books and tennis gear, and left. No food, no water bottle in my new blue VW bug, bought on loan five months earlier. I do not remember leaving the beach, driving through the San Fernando Valley, rising above the L.A. smog. Yet I remember the Ridge Route, a difficult drive in a tiny car with no horsepower to speak of, and trucks roaring up behind or beside me, honking as truck drivers did then, not for me to go faster but because a young woman with flaming red hair was behind the wheel. So odd now to recall those days: no GPS, and me an idiot with maps & directions, plus lousy radio reception on the Ridge and Highway 99. Nothing to distract terrible thoughts of that spring and the horrible men I'd been dating after Mike one's rejection. I tried not to think about what was ahead. Eight weeks in a camp for rich girls.

I had done my semester of student teaching in a high school outside San Francisco with lower class kids of every ethnic background. My classes at Dodson were with marginalized kids. No one used this word then, just said 'disadvantaged'. At the camp I would be spending time with the privileged ones. From years of tennis in Southern California, I was not fond of wealthy kids with their private schools, cashmere sweaters, two newly strung rackets, and tennis shoes that looked always as if new.

In the worst of times, teaching has saved me. I found a profession that took me out of myself and focused my attention on the needs of others. At Dodson Junior High the minority kids burrowed into my fragmented self and kept me from thinking about anything except teaching and Friday night wildness to help me forget a lost love, to use a cliché!

That Sunday at camp, watching Debbie Reynolds step from her limo, I must have been thinking, *What the hell am I doing here?* No problem, however, with the tennis part of it. I had been teaching tennis since high school—from Fullerton to San Francisco, in programs for youth and adults. But living in a cabin with six teens was something else. Having to safeguard and herd them around, listen to their silly chatter, indulge their fears and longings, sing songs by a campfire, have cook-outs, sit down to three meals a day and get fat, and have no liquor. To be there meant I was Miss Desperation. I had taken Dexedrine for the long drive and had a well-coated tongue from it. Worrying about the time, I stopped once for gas on the Ridge and then again in Fresno so I would arrive at the camp with an almost full tank. Did I already have in mind that I would need to escape?

I had no sooner driven down the dusty road to Montecito-Sequoia and found a place to park my VW, when I heard a clanging bell. Lunch time! The absolute last thing I wanted was food. Soon I was seated at a circular table of female counselors. When asked my name, I said, "Gail." No! It was explained that my name had to be related to what I taught. Manic as I felt from the stimulant, I thought "balls" would be a funny answer. Maybe not. I said if the name I gave myself was what I would hear for eight weeks, I needed to think about it. Next, I received instruction in how to pass the food, since I had not been there when everyone else learned how it was done. Counter-clockwise, receiving a platter or serving dish with one hand, crossing it over to the other hand, then passing the platter or dish to the next person. I've always had problems with right and left. And that noon I kept reaching and passing with the wrong hand. The art teacher gave me a sympathetic nod and offered to show me around after lunch. When the meal ended, I was asked to stand and tell everyone in the room my name.

"Volley," I said, amused at my choice because I was a backcourt player and disliked the net.

If Mike had been at lunch that day, I would have noticed his blue eyes and toned body. He must have been eating elsewhere with workers like Jack. What's strange is that I think I had an encounter with Mike and his two brothers one time at Newport Beach where his parents and grandparents rented a cottage each summer, and where my family had a cottage on the ocean front. We used it only in June when there were no renters, or on weekends after renters had moved out and the place had to be cleaned. I often took friends down for the day. Once I was with blond and beautiful Sally, who attracted the attention of a trio of boys, who followed us down the shore. In some subconscious way did I remember this when I saw Mike only an hour or so after my arrival at Montecito-Sequoia?

The art teacher's real name was Anne. She and I left the lodge's dining room after lunch and wandered around, stopping here and there. In one place, and I've no memory of the actual room, Mike was inside. "Gunner, I'd like you to meet Volley," Anne said, then added, "Gunner's going to Air Force pilot training when camp ends."

What provoked me to say, "You look like you have a military personality, Gunner."

Through the years, Mike has related our first meeting to friends and told them what went through his mind. *Who is this bitch?*

On Sunday I met my campers, listened to the orientation for them, attended the first night's dinner, after which each instructor pitched her classes (Mike his), and the campers selected the week's activities. I do remember awakening early that first Monday morning and going to take a shower, putting on a tennis dress, the white of it so odd given the ubiquitous mountain dirt. I realized with a jolt that the only time I would be alone was in the shower and toilet.

By Monday afternoon I felt an acute need to take a drive

and see what was on the road beyond the camp, which I had not driven down on Saturday. My tennis classes were over for the day, and I had no responsibility until I led my campers to the dining hall for dinner. On the only road to the camp, I saw a truck approaching. It was Dr. Barnes. Beside her was someone I had not seen. This person sat tall in the passenger's seat, had very short hair and wore a flannel shirt. Initially I thought he or she worked at the camp. I moved over to allow them to pass my VW and heard honking. Dr. Barnes stuck her hand from the driver's side of the truck and gestured for me to open my window, which was closed because of the dust. "Where are you going?" she called. I told her my classes were over and I was going for a drive. She said to turn around, that I was not allowed to leave the camp except on my day off, Sunday.

Years later in the 70s while teaching high school in the Napa Valley, I devised a unit for sophomore English about 'the' camp experience. *The Butterfly Revolution & Bless the Beasts and the Children* were two popular fiction novels on this subject. I also included William Golding's *Lord of the Flies* to satisfy elitists in the English department. The unit worked well with students. I knew also that I needed to explore the Montecito-Sequoia experience for myself. In these novels, I found affirmation of what I sensed that summer of 1967—namely, the division of campers into two groups, allegedly for the spirit of competition, though the outcome was predetermined as to the winning team.

Red and blue, as I recall, though possibly the teams had names. Carrie Fisher was on the favored team, as was Mike, along with several girls in my cabin who had been to the camp before, which gave them a status that newcomers lacked. This was important because at the end of four weeks a candle ceremony was held at the lake to entice the campers to return the following summer. An incident during that solemn occasion is central to my narrative.

Of the six girls assigned to my cabin, three have vaporized with time. A fourth was from my hometown of Fullerton, the granddaughter of someone my mother knew well. Given the connection of Fullerton and our families, I was wary of this girl, who had been to Montecito-Sequoia before. The oldest girl in the cabin, from a wealthy area of L.A., is someone I appreciated from the first day. Karen, a self-confident adolescent, was good-natured about the eight weeks she would be at camp. She was the one the others in the cabin followed. The exception was Karen number two, whose name I will spell as Karin to avoid confusion. *Mousey* is the word that comes to mind, a word I recall from the 50s, for timid girls with hair hiding their faces. Karin burrowed into her bottom bunk and cried that she wanted to go home. Poor kid! She was scheduled to be at camp for two sessions. Clearly at twenty-four, I was not up for the role of Mommy.

The campers had arrived on Sunday, and that evening after dinner they had to select their activities for the coming week.

Karin had a problem with this, which meant the other five girls and I had to stay in the dining hall until she made her choices, which she refused to do. She wanted me to decide for her. I refused. The self-confident Karen told the undecided Karin to choose the same activities as she (Karen) had, so we could all leave. But Karin was afraid of horses, fearful of water skiing, did not want to shoot a rifle, hated tennis and swimming. "Do fucking arts and crafts all week," Karen said, loud enough for me to hear but not for Dr. Barnes' ears. I remember laughing because the F word was not one that I used, though I heard it often among the marginalized kids I taught.

Karin was the quintessential scapegoat without Piggy's smarts (*Lord of the Flies*). Nothing told her to take an action that would improve her standing among her cabin-mates or with me. She held us up for breakfast, was not showering, put on the same clothes, and whined constantly. As happens, collective dislike of her energized the others and made them a cohesive group. Mousey Karin was only nibbling at her food, so I consulted Bandi, the R.N. on staff, a retired ER nurse from New Mexico. She assured me my camper would get over being homesick and was not going to starve. (In late August when Mike and Jack headed to San Antonio, Texas, for Air Force pilot training, they stopped to see Bandi in Las Cruces, spent the night with her, and learned that she would not return to Dr. Barnes' camp for girls.)

As it happened, at camp the director/professor Dr. Barnes offered a night course through San Jose State. I enrolled because I could use the three credits for the L.A. school district's pay scale. Where I got the fifty-dollar fee I don't know. The charge seemed excessive because California state college tuition was cheap. Maybe the fee included the textbook. Those registered for the twice-weekly course met in Barnes' office & sitting room on the second floor of the lodge. Rumor was she shared "digs" elsewhere with her friend: the tall, gray-haired woman who was in the truck when I had tried to leave camp and was stopped.

Even in a small group, Barnes lectured. But her educational experience was unlike mine. I was working with inner city kids bused to a middle-class junior high in a white neighborhood. From the first class I countered some of Barnes' pronouncements, and her ire at me was obvious. I soon realized her education program at San Jose State was unlike the one I had been in at San Francisco State, a program run by three psychologists. Under their guidance I had developed strengths I did not know I had and was encouraged to confront injustices and the stasis typical of public secondary schools. In the two-semester teaching program, the thirty students met weekly in small encounter groups, underwent sensitivity training, learned how to be direct and forthright, behaviors essential in successful classroom teaching. Everything I learned at SFS was antithetical to the way Barnes, a pontificator, a theorist, a camp owner for rich girls—

taught the small group in her evening class.

Thus far I have described two sides of a determining triangle: Karin and Dr. Barnes. This leaves Mike at the base. Having missed the week orientation before the campers got there, no one went over the rules for counselors. I neither heard nor read, "You are prohibited from dating a fellow counselor." Who might that have been? We were all female. Was the rule to discourage counselors from romantic relationships? Mike, as the rifle instructor, was responsible for only his classes. I have little memory of the males who handled the lake and boating activities, or the horseback riding and stables. Yet from almost the beginning of camp, Mike and I met at night after "lights out" for campers.

On our first day off, Sunday of week one, Mike and I went for a picnic in King's Canyon, along with Jack and a counselor who had ridden with Mike to Montecito-Sequoia. He had stopped in Fresno through a prior arrangement to give her a ride, after driving from Northern California and his home in Los Altos. I have forgotten this counselor's name though I see her in memory: short blond hair, stocky build, big boots, one of the riding instructors.

That Sunday afternoon she annoyed all three of us, though Mike and Jack only looked at her, as if to say it was her last picnic with us. I needed to clarify things! She had told us to be sure to pick up our trash. I retorted that she had no idea who I was, could not know I'd been visiting a cabin in Sequoia National Park since my birth, that I would rather eat a jar of salmon eggs than trash a forest. I probably added an insulting word at the end of my diatribe about her assumption that she needed to tell me to pick up my trash. This young woman, still in college, was taking Barnes' class at night, had attended Montecito-Sequoia as a camper, and was obviously a favorite of the director/owner.

The weeks passed.

The Saturday evening before the fourth week of camp, Mike and I were eating and drinking in a mountain café known for its steaks, when this counselor walked in with a few others from camp. I do not remember what transpired—only that Mike and I were certain she told Barnes about the two of us out on a date. That alone would not have gotten me fired, as she would have had to fire Mike, too. And believe me when I say the director did not want to lose Mike with his good looks and his appeal to campers who swarmed him on Sunday evenings to sign-up for his classes, where they stretched out on mattresses at his rifle range above the two tennis courts. Often, I lobbed balls at him, to the amusement of girls in my tennis classes. In reminiscing with Mike about that summer, I heard something I had forgotten. Mike had offered diving classes too, as an extracurricular activity for campers. Gunner in swim trunks!

The trouble with non-stops, especially those written in an infrared sauna, is that language pours out like the heat I am feeling as I dash these thoughts. How to compress a month of one's life without the length becoming ridiculous? Thus, I will turn memory into an accordion and begin squeezing it in.

As I sit here, in 135 dry heat, the Wild West Day returns, an occasion when everyone was to dress as if a Westerner (which of course we already were). I had packed lightly and quickly for camp, did not own blue jeans, wore tennis dresses for my classes. The art teacher (the counselor I liked) told me to look in the theater/drama room, where I might find something to wear for the Saturday event. What I found was a corset, pleasantly yellowed with age. I hooked it over a tennis dress and stuffed my bra, then devised a Mae West routine to match my outfit (the counselors were to be part of the entertainment). Normally I wore my long hair up or back, a habit from playing competitive tennis. My junior high students had begged me to come to school with my hair "down." The first time I complied (and unknown to me) I was scheduled for my first evaluation from the district office in downtown Los Angeles. A gray-suited, gray-haired woman described me in her report as "unkempt," apparently due to my long-curly red hair. That was how I looked on Wild West Day in a corset, arms and legs bare, all beneath a wild mop of red hair. Dr. Barnes, whose gray hair was permed, looked as if she had lockjaw when she saw me that Saturday. I do know the day involved competitive activities for the two teams, and corset-clad, sandal-wearing Volley was not much help in the tug-of -war.

Mail was important at camp. At some point during the four weeks, I opened a letter from my mother that contained a news article from the *L.A. Times*. I no longer have it so will make up the caption. *U.C.L.A. Student Sets Herself on Fire.* Not my mother's usual clipped articles about losing weight or being less argumentative. Then I saw the name Nancy, a classmate from Fullerton, a particularly sad case, someone I could write a long story about. Nancy was a twin, whose brother in high school had gone to Europe under a program for foreign exchange students. Nancy was not in her brother's accelerated classes. After high school she went off to the Mid-West to a posh finishing school; and after two years there, attended USC briefly. I think she left after her first semester following an unsuccessful sorority rush.

During my junior year in high school, my mother had come home one late afternoon from the hospital where she was an admitting clerk. She told me that I was not to tell anyone that Nancy had arrived by ambulance during the night after ingesting a bottle of aspirin. Her stomach had been pumped before she was released to her parents. And now, in late June of 1967, Nancy had sat on the UCLA campus, poured gasoline from her head to her feet, ignited her petrol-soaked clothing, and died in a hospital hours later. I remember taking the article to a large rock near my cabin and sitting there. Many of us in junior high and high school, including me, had been bloody awful to Nancy. I recalled the time she had paid for an expensive dinner for three of us in Los Angeles and provided tickets for a premier movie. The film's title eludes me but not Nancy's acute need to buy friendship. She had attempted to play tennis and been terrible at it, taken dance and failed miserably. I had known Nancy since junior high and now she was dead. I sat on the rock and heard my campers calling me. It was 'cook out' time, a night off for the kitchen staff, a test of camper skills: build a fire, peel the potatoes and carrots, cube the meat, slice the onions, and cook the meal in foil over coals. Only I kept looking at the fire and could not get Nancy out of my mind. Death by fire? If I did not feel any emotion, I could imagine the desperation which drove Nancy to such a violent act.

Karen must have sensed that something was not right with me and took over. I mention this because in a sense the news about Nancy's death figures later, when I was barreling in my VW in King's Canyon, trying to keep Mike in view as he sped down the mountain in his new Cougar.

Unlike Nancy who tried so hard to belong, camper Karin remained on the periphery, her only status to be a pain in the ass from morning to night. Yet ironically, she reached a level of acceptance with all of us in the most bizarre way on the night before the four-week session ended. This was the night of the candle-lighting ceremony with its tiny trials, such as crossing water by walking on logs to reach the sacred grounds where songs would be sung. There, the past month's successes would be acclaimed, with candles lighted, which were to be re-lit at Christmas or Hanukkah.

I knew Karin was uncoordinated. I assumed this was why she scorned sports and avoided physical activities. But it was not as if we were crossing rolling logs that evening. Caution and safety were foremost at the camp. The logs were big ones, which someone could walk on almost normally. No one pushed Karin. No one tripped her. But she fell off the log into the water. We were the last group to cross, and I cannot explain what happened. But this poor kid achieved a moment of acceptance in her clumsy fall. The five against Karin were suddenly in sympathy with her. And instead of bawling or quitting (I offered to take her back to the cabin so she could change clothes), she wanted to be with the others. Our assigned place at the ceremony was off to the side but in the front row. I do not recall which of the six began laughing first, not in derision but because Karin was one of them. And they could not stop laughing, which provided enormous release of tension: four weeks together, homesickness, constant activities, bad beds, no telephones, monotonous food. Yet now the scapegoat sat among them, wet and muddied, laughing for the first time in four weeks. I tried to silence them. But one would chuckle, and the crazy laughter would begin again, disrupting a staged ceremony designed to guarantee that campers returned to Montecito-Sequoia the following summer.

The four-week girls left the following morning. I've no memory of what the eight-week campers did while their counselors wrote 'camp reports'—both for those girls who left on Saturday and those who remained for another session. The six letters took me no time at all. I had been told to turn them in by mid-afternoon. I will not re-create a scene I do not see in detail. I only know that I went to Barnes' office in the lodge and put my letters on her desk. We had been told not to sign them until the director had read and approved each one. She glanced over my six quickly, made a comment about me being an English teacher, then told me I was no longer needed and could leave. Only she did not mean leave her office. I remember saying, "Are you firing me?" Indeed, she was! I was expected to pack and leave *now.* Mike and I cannot recall how we received our pay for the first session of camp. I do remember asking Barnes to refund the $50.00 for the course I would not be able to complete. She told me to take the matter up with San Jose State, which I did, unsuccessfully. Then Barnes told me to sign the six letters before I left her office. I refused. "You forge them," I said.

I found Mike somewhere and told him I had been fired. My life turned on that moment, as it had before and would again so many times in the next fifty years. He never hesitated. "Then I'll quit too." He went to Barnes' office, said if Volley was leaving, so was he. "Fine," she told him.

A combination of cheek and financial desperation made us

stay for dinner, with Karen seated beside me, begging that we take her with us. "That's considered kidnapping," we told her. It was not the last time we saw Karen, as she attended our wedding the following June.

Mike and I left Montecito-Sequoia in the early evening—he in his new white Cougar and me in my blue bug, which was no match for his ease of speed down the mountain. Our plan was to stop at a gas station after our descent, as I had a ten-dollar coupon for Chevron, a birthday gift from my grandmother.

What, I wonder, was going through my mind, as I tried to keep Mike's Cougar within sight, exceeding in my car a reasonable speed on curves, especially with no guard rail between the two-lane road and the deep King's Canyon. In high school my brother Barry had been a passenger in a VW that too quickly entered a freeway off-ramp and rolled off, leaving four of them upside down but uninjured. Not so with the VW's crushed roof. Later Barry forgot about curves and excessive speed. On his way to our family's cabin in the Sequoias, he had rolled his VW bug. A passerby stopped and helped him upright the tiny car and he drove on, his roof dented but not crushed. Had Barry warned me about braking in a sudden turn in a VW bug?

Once, when I was ten during our yearly summer vacation at Newport Beach, I had been told to stay out of the surf because the tide was too high. I went body surfing anyway, and a huge wave swallowed me. I have never forgotten its force, turning me over and over, something in me knowing to succumb to its power and allow the wave to do with my body whatever it wanted. I ended up on the shore—rubbed raw, gulping, frightened, knowing not to tell my mother what had happened.

That July evening in King's Canyon I came around a curve much too fast, felt the VW begin its rotation like the Magic Teacup ride at Disneyland: a full spin, a masterful, mechanical pirouette. "Oh well, what the hell," went through my mind, of flying downward into the canyon, dying in a blaze like Nancy. I never touched the brake and ended up where I had begun, driving downward, only now very slowly. At the gas station below, Mike asked what had taken me so long to get off the mountain. I've no idea what I said.

Yet years later when I reread E.M. Forster's *Passage to India*, a novel I loved in college, I noticed something that had not penetrated before. Miss Quested is in an automobile accident on a crowded road in India but the passengers escape harm. She declares, "I was not frightened at all." I no longer have a copy of this beloved novel, and I quote from memory that Aziz says: "To not be afraid is the height of folly, Miss Quested."

No irony, dear daughters, that folly rhymes with Volley. Yet be of great joy that I had the good sense and sanity to marry your father on June 28th, 1968, after which I sent a wedding announcement to Dr. Barnes. Ah, life!

Robert Theron Wilson

W hile living in Malaysia from 1987 to 1990, I became aware of ancestral shrines. At the time of death in a Chinese family, the departure was in body only, with the person's memory and spirit honored at a designated place in the home. My own family might have wondered why I framed so many old photographs and hung them on walls in our Virginia residence in the mid-90s. In some small way I, a migrant in time, was trying to honor the departed ones and remind myself that I descended from those who surrounded me. By my closet door, which I opened numerous times a day, I placed a photograph of my father taken in his youth at the University of Southern California, on the same courts where I had played tennis. In the photo my father is dressed in tennis attire of his era. One sleeve of his shirt is rolled in the style of his tennis hero, Bill Tilden. This famous player, acknowledged as the master of spin, died dishonored and disgraced because, in those closeted times, he was a gay man. I don't suppose my father knew of Tilden's sexual preference. What he admired was the man's elegance and skill as a tennis player.

My father, Robert Theron Wilson, died on June 10, 1986. All these many years later his death leaves me with guilt that I had not flown to California to be with him. At the time my family of four had tickets for California following our planned trip to Germany. Husband Mike had weeks to fill between his graduation from Air War College in Alabama and reporting to the Pentagon. We also needed to find a house to rent. All this intervened with returning to California earlier than planned. We were there for my father's funeral instead of when he died. In retrospect, it all seems misguided and insensitive.

The day my father died I was in a German village, where a friend from Ramstein Air Force Base had tracked me down, after the Red Cross notified her of Robert Theron Wilson's death. Distance has made me realize what I couldn't feel that day, and distance has helped me see my father as a youthful mind had not seen him. I would like to think the eternal struggle in most of us to spite a parent or to please a parent no longer exists in me. But the other day while playing tennis, I said aloud, "I am going to be the best 80-year-old female player in the USA." Then I laughed and thought how much those words rang a rusty bell of wanting to say to my father, "This championship is for you, Dad."

Of his early life my father seldom spoke. Or if he did speak about his boyhood in Arkansas, I don't recall the stories. I only know his family left Gotham, Arkansas, when he was young. Later in life, my aunt Erin, his older sister, liked to visit Arkansas, and she talked openly about the life she remembered there. But I don't recall my father saying, "When I lived in Arkansas," perhaps because of embarrassment about his poor rural past.

I now wish I knew more about my father's life as a boy. There are no photos. And if there were photographs, they disappeared after my Grandmother Wilson's death in 1962. I know my father loved to fish and he loved to hunt. Had he, like Jody Baxter in *The Yearling*, gone hunting with his father in Arkansas? My father loved games like poker and cribbage, and sports of all kinds: horseshoes, bowling, golf, and tennis. What games and sports had he played as a child? What had the Wilson family raised and grown on their farm? Later in life, Dad liked to shoot quail and pheasant, which we ate. But not in Pauma Valley, his final home, where he relished his quail, which came each late afternoon for seed. He loved his German shepherd Sage, too. Did he have a dog as a boy? I seem to recall stories about dogs but can't remember them. He also liked vegetable gardens and took pride in the tomatoes he grew in Pauma, along with the avocado and grapefruit groves he maintained on his small ranch.

When I was seven, we had moved from a farmhouse in Anaheim, California, and rented a new house in nearby Fullerton. I hated that 1950s track house and have few memories of Father inside it. Instead, I see him in the backyard, planting a garden. In a child's memory it is a huge garden with rows of carrots, potatoes, plentiful green beans, and tomato plants. I think of my father as a character from Jonathan Swift, one like Gulliver who preferred horses in the barn to people. Swift reserved his love for individuals and claimed to hate mankind. That's something my father might have said, although in his case he loved nature most of all. If he drew a bad hand and an unexpected storm wiped out his avocado crop, it was the life of a farmer and he accepted Mother Nature's whims stoically. Yet if Father had to deal with a fool, then life wasn't okay. And from my father's view, the chance of colliding with fools was an everyday occurrence, unless a person separated himself from them.

What else did my father love besides Mother Nature and the Pacific Ocean? Horse races. On Malvern Avenue in Fullerton, our residence after the dreadful track house, we would sit in the kitchen and listen to the Santa Anita races on the radio. We would have placed our small bets that morning after consulting the sporting green in the *L.A. Times*. I aways looked for Willie Shoemaker's name and placed my dime on whatever horse he was riding. Robert Theron Wilson liked betting and he liked winning. But I grew up thinking that if I didn't win, I was a loser; and if I was a loser, then I wasn't to be respected, and if I wasn't respected, then I wasn't loved. Like my father, I'm a tangled complex. But now I love my father for this and so much more.

At the time of his death, I could not believe Father would not pull through. He had been close to death before. When I was thirteen, his appendix ruptured. He entered the hospital at 170 pounds and left at 125, his muscles hanging from his arms and legs. Then in June 1960 before my senior year in high school, he almost bled to death in a strawberry field from a perforated artery to his stomach. Which is why over two decades later in 1983, at the time of his heart surgery, I felt a frightening urgency to see him. Mike, the girls and I had left Germany that summer, were visiting family in Michigan, and planning to head to California by car. I awakened one morning in Michigan and said I had to fly to California. I flew there that same day. The following one I remember standing beside Dad's bed and taking his hand, which felt so thin and dry. He opened his eyes and saw me, said, "Gail," with an emotion I seldom heard in his voice. I hadn't seen him for three years, and the last view had been at a distance. He hadn't come up from his avocado grove to say good-bye and I hadn't walked down. The same old tension and stupidity characterizing our farewell. But he survived the surgery in 1983, was given a new heart valve compliments of a pig, which took him back to his southern roots on a farm. For the next year or two, he seemed well but then slipped into a terrible state. My family and I were living in Alabama that year, and Mother came to visit us in late spring, leaving Father alone. No one knew what was wrong with him. He would not get up to work on the ranch, had sores on his body, even his teeth were infected. At the time of his death, hospital personnel refused the autopsy my mother asked to have done. Then a California state senator died of AIDS. What was that? My father, like the senator and Arthur Ashe, was given tainted blood during heart surgery.

Years after Father's death, I wrote a short piece about fishing with my father. Then in 2004 when I moved to the Northern Neck of Virginia, I impulsively adopted a roadway in his memory, and wrote an essay about the experience published in *Pleasant Living*, a regional periodical (see page 131).

On Fishing and Writing

My father, like many Southerners, was a storyteller. Yet hard times had forced his family to move from Arkansas to California, to a land where people had less time to tell stories. Although I wasn't outwardly close to my father, when I turned ten and felt estranged from my mother, I was drawn to him. Those were the years when we spent summer vacations at Newport Beach in southern California, and where each evening after the sun had set, my father took his pole and went down to the ocean to fish.

Our actual preparation for fishing had begun in early morning. I still see Father as I saw him then: waiting for the tide to ebb, then pulling a wire crab catcher back and forth as waves receded from the shore. His effort of pulling the catcher through the heavy wet sand created an odd swizzle in his legs and hips. After he dumped the catcher's contents on dry sand, I joined the search for bait. We tossed the hard-shelled crabs back toward the sea and watched them disappear into the wet sand. The unfortunate soft-shelled crabs became the bait for that night's fishing.

Never a contented man in the world of commerce, Father sat peacefully near the water's edge. There beneath the stars he seldom spoke. From those wordless hours I learned that fishing is a time to sit and enjoy the lovely wetness the sea air brings. Night after night my father cast his line into the Pacific Ocean, assuring me the fish were out there, just waiting to bite. Yet looking away from the tip for even a moment might mean missing a strike. The word sounded so impressive to my youthful ear, though a strike was only a tiny movement in the pole's tip.

The wait always seemed endless. Then suddenly the tip would move slightly, and my father would spring from the sand, grab the pole from its stake, and begin to reel in his catch. More than anything I loved to watch the pole arch and straighten. My excitement was always comingled with fear the pole might snap. Often Father reeled in an empty line or thought he had a large fish, which turned out to be a shovel-nosed shark. Father disliked sharks and expressed disgust when he cut one from his line. But he admired the other fish he caught and taught me to identify their markings. As a ten-year-old, eating a fried perch for breakfast confirmed that my father was a fine fisherman. It didn't matter that his picture never appeared in the local paper for having caught the largest fish at Newport Beach. If my father dreamed of fishing fame, the absence of it never kept him from casting his line into the sea.

After my father's death, I found a journal he kept as a young man when he boarded a tramp steamer as crew to get to Europe where he traveled throughout the continent. These words opened an unknown window into his life. I do know my father would be proud that I'm not a soft-shell crab and haven't shed tears over "rejection" of my writing. Instead, I have regarded the sea for writers as enormous. And true to my father's example as a fisherman, I've had lots of small bites, occasionally a good-sized one, even snagged a big one in a national magazine once. My first book provided royalties for twenty years, another was given a grant, and at present I have four books in print.

Yet what has been important? The act of writing itself.

Only now do I understand why Father abandoned a world of commotion for one of solitude, and why he cast his line into the sea even when it came back empty. Now I understand his dislike of shovel-nose sharks, as I've reeled in some of those from the writer's sea. But that's not all I've learned from those nights spent fishing with my father. Now I understand about the need to be attentive while fishing or writing. I've also learned that even if you have patience and conviction and concentration, the elusive fish often gets away. This is what Ernest Hemingway and his old man Santiago knew, and what my father tried to teach me without words. If the act itself is an affirmation, then there's no end to it.

You keep casting and you keep watching and sometimes when you would rather look past the tip to the stars, you bring your eyes back to that fixed point. And if anything should strike in those quiet moments, you will be there, waiting.

My father surf-fishing at Newport Beach, California.

Billie Jean King

August 6, 2022
Dear Billie Jean,
This is a voice from your Southern California past, from a tennis player you might not remember. Last year I cut an article from the *WSJ Review* (August 14-15). And just now, this Saturday morning in the Northern Neck of Virginia, I have reread this article about you. It is strange, at least to me, that two So-Cal tennis playing 'girls' ended up in Virginia so late in life. One of fame, the other a "nobody," who despite this has decided to write tennis recollections for her daughters. I recently reminded Michelle, an Army brigadier general, that she would not exist were it not for tennis. From the age of 10 to 79, this sport has been woven into my life. I still play, hitting four times a week with much younger men, and running on two

new knees, compliments of a fine Richmond orthopedic, Dr. William Nordt. I am fortunate to live near Kilmarnock and the Indian Creek Country Club, which has an indoor tennis facility and a fine pro named George Christoforatos.

This morning I remembered that my first ever tournament final was in Whittier, California, against you. We were in seventh grade then and products of public courts & city recreation programs. Only I caught a flu two days before the Whittier final and had to default. A few years later I might have played you in the National Hardcourt championships in June of 1960, were it not for a broken foot, which sent me home from Burlingame to Fullerton. My doubles partner, Mary Jo Conger, played you in the semi-finals that June. Then she traveled on to Oregon, Washington, and Canada. That summer my tennis aspirations ended. But later, while at USC, our team practiced from time to time with you and L.A. State's team.

Out USC tennis coach was instrumental in the establishment of Title 9 for women's sports. In spring 1964, our team participated in the first inclusion of female players in the PAC-8 tennis tournament, held at Stanford University that year. Earlier, around 1963, you and I were housed together in a sorority at University of Arizona. By then you had been to Wimbledon. I remember one morning over breakfast, asking to hear all about playing there. Yet in the Arizona collegiate tournament that year, you lost to Ann Kinney from San Diego in the first round. I had lost in the first round, too. This meant you and I had to play in the consolation draw against each other. I had watched Ann (a fellow redhead) beat you by dinking. I remember saying to you that we were going to hit the ball and have a good match. And we did. You won, of course!

I have not forgotten a day at a summer tournament in La Jolla in 1958 or 59, when you told a group of us that you were going to be the best woman tennis player in the world. We did not doubt it. This has been your legacy, Billie Jean, along with all you have done for women's tennis. The other day a good friend received a call from her precocious three-year-old granddaughter in Boston. Noa told her grandmother that she liked *The Little Feminist*, and she repeated your name and Sally Ride's. My friend loved this and related it to me yesterday during her weekly tennis session with me at Indian Creek.

Last fall in Richmond's Costco, I saw your book and read through it while my husband did the monthly shopping. While reading about your early years in California, I decided to write a nobody's book about tennis. Why? Because everything in my life since age ten has been connected to this sport. And writing about tennis is a way to jettison a box of old clippings which moved with me throughout the United States and five other countries. More than anything I wish to honor my father, whose sagacity to make me a tennis player has made all the difference in my life.

I know you are busy in all kinds of ways, especially as the U.S. Open approaches. I do not know how often you are in Richmond, but I am there frequently. Do you still get out and play tennis? How I would love to hit with you one more time. I recall from a television interview at one slam or the other, that both of your knees had been replaced. I am enclosing a card with my website. Not that I look as I did when you knew me with red hair and freckles. Please know of my continuing respect for all you have done, Ms. Billie Jean Moffitt King.

Good thoughts to you, Gail Wilson Kenna

Post Script: After I wrote this letter, I pulled three clippings from the aforementioned box.

First clipping: Constantine (Tanny) Tanasecu was my coach for several years after he watched me play this match in Ventura. His son Gino was one of the most beautiful players I ever saw in So Cal. In college he played for UCLA, along with Arthur Ashe. Don't we both appreciate Arthur's statue on Monument Avenue in Richmond? The Confederate Generals are gone but the city's famous tennis player remains.

The second clipping is from Ojai in 1964. Dennis Ralston, as you know, died a few years ago. Charles Rombeau died shortly after leaving USC. Rafael Osuna is not pictured. But he died in a plane crash not long after that same year. Upsetting to

Bond Falls to Tanasescu In Junior Tennis Upset

TOP-SEEDED Bill Bond of La Jolla was knocked off by un-ranked Eugen Tanasescu of Los Angeles in a three-set surprise that highlighted yesterday's action in the 12th annual Ventura Junior Tennis Championships.

Tanasescu, pulling his surprise in the 15-under singles, took a 6-3, 3-6, 6-4 victory over Bond, winner of that event at this year's Ojai tournament. Tanasescu also gained the semifinals of the 13-under, where he is top-seeded, with a 6-0, 6-0 shutout of Craig Baise.

In another upset, second-seeded Ann Heck of Ventura bowed to Gail Wilson, 6-1, 3-6, 6-4, in the quarterfinals of the girls 13-under singles.

Seeded players advanced in all other events.

Ramsey Earnhart of Ventura gained the quarterfinals in the junior boys competition with a tight 7-5, 4-6, 6-1 victory over George Conway of Santa Monica,

TENNIS TIME—Under traditionally cloudy skies, Ojai Valley Tennis Tournament opened its 64th annual stand today, drawing top players including, left to right, Linda Lee Crosby, Charles Rombeau, Gail Wilson, Dennis Ralston, Liz Jones—all of USC—and Charles Pasarell, top tennis player at UCLA and rated No. 10 player in the nation. Matches will continue through Sunday.

think of these early deaths on the USC team. But Charlie Pasarell is alive. I met him again after Ojai at Randolph Air Force Base in Texas the summer of 1968. He had not completed UCLA, which meant he was enlisted in the military, not an Army officer like Ashe. But he was playing the summer circuit in 1968, along with a USAF player. I replaced this fellow that summer as the base tennis teacher. I was at Randolph because I had married a USAF student-pilot. I only met Mike because of a job teaching tennis in 1967 at a California camp for girls in King's Canyon where we both worked.

This clipping from Ojai makes me wonder if you remember Linda Lou Crosby. Her sister, Cathy Lee, became a movie actress.

The other woman in the photo was not at USC. Denny is leaning toward me, asking if I would like to play poker that evening. The game included Arthur Ashe that night, the most intelligent male tennis player I ever met. A favorite book of mine is *Levels of the Game*, by John McPhee. I bet you have read this book about the Ashe & Clark

Mary Jo Conger in Tourney Semi-Finals

BURLINGAME — Mary Jo Conger reached the semi-finals today, in the National Junior Hardcourt Tennis Championships. She was due to face seeded Billie Jean Moffitt of Long Beach.

Gail Wilson, who competed earlier this week at the tourney, was due to reach home today, following her withdrawl from the match, due to her broken foot bone, received in match play. Next week, Mary Jo leaves for a tourney in Washington.

Graebner semi-final match at Forest Hills in 1968. How McPhee wove a tennis match into a book about privilege, politics, and human behavior is masterful. My father like Ashe, died of complications from heart surgery and HIV infected blood.

The third clipping includes your name. You were in the stands when I fell and broke five bones in my left foot. I finished the match and won. By midnight I had a cast. Hard to believe I was housed in the home of two physicians, when few women were medical doctors then. It was the first time ever I had fallen on a tennis court. This occurred during the same hour when my father began vomiting blood in a strawberry field near Newport Beach. An undetected ulcer had perforated an artery and he almost died the summer of 1960. I think of this as the beginning of mysterious moments in life related to tennis.

I doubt this letter will reach you at your house in Richmond. I've no idea how often you are there or if mail is delivered to you. Probably not. No matter, as I have enjoyed recalling past connections with you.   – Gail Wilson Kenna

Nothing Much Remains the Same

In the early 1970s in California's Napa Valley, I taught high school English and played a lot of tennis. I also read Alvin Toffler's *Future Shock*. At the time in 1971, my husband Mike, a USAF pilot, went to Thailand during the Vietnam war. Why do I mention Toffler? Because he explained future shock through culture shock, which is what I experienced in Thailand when I visited Mike for his R & R. Never in my life had I wanted to enter a bar at 10 a.m. and have a gin and tonic. In bustling Bangkok, with no slots in my head for Asian culture, I felt shockingly disoriented. That's when I began to grasp Toffler's *Future Shock* and took note of a suggestion he made in the book. He advised the reader to find something in life that would not be subject to technology's increasingly rapid rate of change. At the time I hoped the sport of tennis would be that unchanging 'something' in my life.

Now in 2022, I am writing these words many months after watching this year's Wimbledon. The court size remains the same. Tennis continues to be played on hardcourts, clay, and grass. The balls are the same size, though a softer one is available for youngsters new to the sport, along with smaller racquets. Those did not exist for me at age ten in 1953. I went to my first tennis lesson with my father's heavy racquet and its too large grip. Eventually, white balls turned into yellow ones, and technology got hold of the racquets. I so wish I'd kept one of my many wood frames: Spaulding, Dunlop, Wilson. Not until 1987 did I bid wood good-bye and switch to a Wilson composite. Twenty years earlier, my brother had given me the Jimmy Connor wire racquet for Christmas. I quickly gave up trying to hit with it. Yet that odd racquet forecast what was to come with new tennis technology. Since 1987 I have been through different Wilson and Babolat racquets with varying head sizes. Now I'm using a new brand of tennis racquet, a Tecnifibre, and I like it best of all.

When I think back to Napa and playing competitive tennis, I recall watching 16-year-old Chris Evert arrive on the tennis scene at the U.S. Open in 1971 with her powder-puff serve. At the time, I could have practiced tennis with any female player competing in the Grand Slams, as no women smashed the ball then with the velocity of today's players and racquets. I don't mean to say the female players wouldn't have killed me in a match. Yet I would have been able to hit with the best of them.

Something else has changed besides racquets. In all my years of playing competitive tennis, I never heard players emit sounds as they do now, especially female players. Non-players might not understand the problem with grunts and screams. Seeing the ball is essential, but hearing the ball leave an opponent's racquet is also crucial to reading a shot. Unfortunately, this habit of players making loud noises while hitting balls has multiplied like worms after a heavy rain, the gardener in me notes.

Roger Federer, one of the truly great players, if not the best male player ever, did not make vocal sounds when he hit the ball. For decades until the Pandemic, I loved watching Federer play. His final match in London this year on September 23rd left me bereft. I'd so wanted Roger and Rafael Nadal to win against the U.S. team of Tiafoe and Sock. One ace on Federer's serve would have done it. *Oh, please, let Federer leave the sport he loves with an untouchable serve.* But his first serve on match point missed the center line. Instead of holding serve, he and Rafa lost that game. Then they lost the third-set's tiebreaker. Yet Federer hit a volley I will not forget, with his racquet touching the ball as it dropped over the net, his return zipping parallel along the width of the court and dropping into the opponent's alley beyond reach. Federer's perfect touch was a thing of beauty, along with his amazement and delight at his shot.

Once on television I heard John McEnroe say of Roger Federer, "We'll never see a player this beautiful again." Yes, Roger was beauty in motion, and his grace extended to his comportment on and off the court. That recent September 23rd evening in London, during an interview with Jim Courier, the intelligent & gifted Roger, openly showed his emotions, trying to maintain control and not breakdown. I watched and listened and silently wept.

I thought of being in Sri Lanka in 2008, teaching English that July for my daughter Bonnie's NGO organization, one headquartered in Colombo. One evening I went with her to a U.N. party, being held to watch the Federer-Nadal Wimbledon final. For the most part it was a young crowd and I positioned myself close to the television. Across the room was an older man from Switzerland, mouthing off. "Oh, that Federer. So overrated. Nadal will 'kheel' him in straight sets." He kept blabbering in his heavy Swiss, French accent. Bonnie later told me she knew I wasn't going to keep my mouth shut. I finally said, "You obviously don't play tennis and don't know what the hell you're talking about." Yet it did appear that Roger was going to be beat badly. At some point the television reception was lost. Nadal was ahead by two sets, with the Swiss fellow ragging me about Federer. Bonnie and I left the party. The following morning she came to my room with the latest news. The 2008 Wimbledon final had lasted four hours and 48 minutes, and Rafael Nadal won 9-7 in the fifth set. When the total points were tallied, Nadal had won by one point.

Each year the players get younger and hit harder. It is unlikely that many of them will be playing competitive tennis at 41, Federer's age of retirement. A player like Australian Ken Rosewall kept playing professional tennis until age 43, and even attempted a comeback at 47. At the age of 40 he lost the Wimbledon finals to Jimmy Connors. This slam eluded Rosewall, who was a picture of grace and beauty at 5'7" and 148 pounds, hitting his perfect slice backhand, with nothing in his tennis form to injure his body, unlike today.

One change in tennis is the way strokes are executed in open stances, the wacky grips players use, racquets whipped around the head like Nadal's, elbows often leading, odd positions with extreme torque, players jumping into the air to reach big top-spin balls, plus serves that clock the highest reaches of miles per hour, right up there with my Miata's 140 speedometer. I cannot imagine a serve of this speed sent from great height. Will tennis for men and woman become a discouragement to those who are not six feet and above? Maybe tennis should have competition based on height the way boxing does for weight. Will the rules need to change? Eliminate the 'let' on the serve? Allow a player only one serve?

Another change in tennis has been scoring. The longest set I ever played went to 16-14. Later tie breakers arrived. When a set reached 6 all, the 7 point "breaker" is played. And in 2023, all four Grand Slams will have a ten-point tie breaker for the final set. Women will continue to play best of three set matches while men still face five sets in the Slams. Does this need to change? Is it unfair to men who play best of five sets to receive the same size purse as women who play three sets?

Money in tennis is the greatest change of all. The world's number one female player for 2022, Iga Swiatek from Poland, ends the year with $9,875,525 prize money, according to a November 18th article in the *Wall Street Journal.* This article sent me to the internet where I learned Billie Jean King is worth twenty million dollars. Yet back in our mutual college days, she at L.A. State and me at USC, no scholarships were available for women athletes. As said before, two separate tennis worlds from then to now; and I can only imagine what is ahead in the sport.

I do admit to relishing Wimbledon where the ruckus that characterizes the U.S. Open is disallowed. Call me hopelessly old school, but I love Wimbledon where white clothing prevails. No leopard prints or garish colors allowed. I was feeling smug that white attire has not changed, until a few days ago when a change was announced for the 2023 Wimbledon. Women players may wear colored shorts or bloomers beneath their white dresses and avert red blood showing on white, a concern that male players do not face.

Just now, writing concluding thoughts, an image returned of Arthur Ashe. It is 1968 and he crosses the lawn at Forest Hills to play the men's final against Tom Okker. Ashe would be the first African American to win this title, and that year was the first time when both amateur and professionals competed for the national championship. As Ashe strides in, he has two racquets. He carries no bag with a dozen racquets as they do today. He has no Player's box, shown repeatedly these days during televised matches. The inhabitants of the box vary, but some are loaded with a coach, trainer, physical therapist, psychologist, family, and friends.

In 1968, Ashe was in the U.S. Army, and for the fourteen-day tournament, his military payment (*per diem*) was $20.00. Ashe won the title, but the $14,000 for winning the championship went to his opponent, a professional player.

If you love tennis, as I do, a must read is *Levels of the Game*, by the brilliant writer, John McPhee, about the 1968 semi-final match between Ashe and Clark Graebner. A point-by-point analysis is given. But the book is about something much larger than the match alone. *Levels of the Game* is considered the best tennis book ever written.

Admittedly, I am a relic of another age. Yet at almost 80, I am a body in motion on a tennis court. The sport has remained that constant "something" in my life; and I am grateful from my head to my feet for the seventy years I have swung a tennis racquet.

Set Two

The Summer of Watergate

Today, January 20th, 2021, watching Donald Trump depart the White House, I recalled the summer of Watergate with its lies, fired special prosecutor, incriminating tapes, and more. Memory grabs deeply at my throat. I see Thad, a more physically fit man than Trump. By now he must be dead unless he had his body frozen for a later return.

My memory of this man, using a fictional name, begins with bubble gum. One stifling summer day in California's Napa Valley, playing tennis on public courts, I stepped in a melting wad of purple bubble gum that clung to the sole of my tennis shoe. I tried to pull the gum off, but the smell of grape flavoring, the nauseating artificial kind, stayed on my fingers. I shouted across the net to my tennis partner that I needed a break.

"Do you think they ever clean these courts?" I asked, sitting down. Nell, on a nearby bench, was rolling moist dirt from her calves into miniature tootsie rolls. She looked up and laughed. Then forgetting the broken strings of her past and mine, I mentioned again my idea of finding a private court in the valley where we could practice.

No recounted memory without backstory.

If I had not fallen during the National Junior Hardcourt Championships in Burlingame, California, and broken my foot, I might have made a name for myself in tennis like Billie Jean

71

Moffitt, who was in the stands that day. Nell's accident had been more dramatic than mine. She had flown from a motorcycle in Berkeley and injured her back, then worn a brace in competition before she stored her rackets, along with her father's dream of reproducing Little Mo. Maureen Connolly had been on my father's mind, too. Whenever he and I practiced, Father would not let me quit until I knocked down the targets he positioned on the court. That habit of hitting a target began early in life, when I learned to drop a ball and whack whatever Father directed me to hit. Sometimes he would turn his back and bend over. "Think you can hit that?" By the time I was winning tournaments in Southern California, the target was considerably smaller than Father's backside.

One Monday during the summer of Watergate, shortly after the incident with the bubble gum, I was watching the televised Senate hearings. From my college days at the University of Southern California, I knew several of the White House conspirators. Gordon was walking into the Senate chamber when I heard the telephone ring in the kitchen.

I told my tennis partner Nell to make it fast, that an old friend was testifying before the Watergate Committee. She asked if I had heard of Thad Symington, a big shot who owned a chain of steak restaurants that stretched from Kansas to San Francisco. The name meant nothing, but the fantastic court that Nell described intrigued me.

"Thad isn't any good," she said. "But he wants to play you this afternoon before he agrees to let us use his court."

"What's the rush?"

"I thought you would be excited. I've never seen a court like this."

"What's the catch?"

"A few sets of singles when he's here on long weekends."

I hated to play when the sun was intense and reminded Nell of this. But she pleaded.

"Okay," I said, "if it won't take long to beat him."

"He talks a lot."

"What's that mean?" I said, untangling the phone cord that had twisted around my wrist.

"Just don't let him beat you."

"You said he isn't any good."

"He isn't. But he doesn't like to lose."

With wells in the Napa Valley drying up in August, dead foliage was everywhere until I turned onto Country Club Drive and saw rain birds spraying water on lush green fairways. I drove slowly, scanning house numbers on decorated mailboxes. At a bend in the road, I saw the tennis court and eased into a circular driveway. A canyon away on Soda Creek, abundant oaks shaded my cottage. Here the native oaks had been uprooted. I stepped from the car and felt a ruthless sun. The day was already overheated. Gordon involved in Watergate? On television he had looked as I remembered him at USC: tall and lean, straight blond hair falling across one side of his handsome face. Even under the apparent strain of testifying, he had been the sincere Gordon I knew and liked in college.

Glancing toward the house, I caught my reflection in the

large kitchen window. I had forgotten sunscreen and needed to win quickly or pay in blistered skin. I turned from the window and followed a bark path to the tennis court, heard splashing, walked closer, and saw a black-bottomed swimming pool—oddly sinister in mid-day light. Two boys noticed me, stopped pushing water at each other, and sent it toward a small girl standing near the pool. "Daddy," she cried, sending her plea upward to an office where a man sat at a desk near an open door.

"My dad's gonna beat you," the older boy taunted.

"Your dad's a good player?"

The boy swam to the pool edge near me.

"Yeah," he said, displaying a mouthful of braces. "He always wins."

"Not this morning?"

"Dad didn't lose! You gotta play a whole match to lose."

"News to me," I laughed, pointing to the office. "Is your father making a telephone call?"

"He's not on the phone. He's listening to his secretary."

I saw only one person and asked if the secretary was invisible.

"Don't you know what an electric secretary is?"

The boy climbed from the pool, cupped wet hands, and shouted, "Hey, Dad."

A man with a bare chest and thinning blond hair came to the doorway and called that he would be down in a minute.

I walked around the pool to the base of the stairs. It was more than a few minutes before Thad came down, extended his hand, and held mine a bit too long. "Hey, Nell didn't tell me you were a beautiful redhead." He pointed to the pool. "Good looking kids, aren't they? Come on. I'll show you around."

Beyond the large beds of summer annuals, a man-made creek ran between Thad's property and the closest fairway. A rope bridge was strung across the water, and a shiny tire hung from the branch of a surviving oak. Behind my cottage the creek was dry and would remain that way until the winter rains began.

"What do you think of this lay-out?" Thad asked. "My kids love telling their San Francisco friends about life in the country. Now for the best part of the tour!"

He reached for my elbow, as if I needed to be led up the path. By the court's rear gate he bent, gesturing for me to get down beside him. Running his hand over the surface, he said to touch it. "Ever feel a court this smooth or see one this blue?"

I said my rackets were in the car and headed up the path to get them.

Thad was practicing his serve on the shady side when I returned.

"I hear you're so good you don't need a warm-up. Serve 'em up," he called from the shade.

"Aren't we spinning for serve?'

"Hey, I'm giving you an advantage."

Sure, I thought, with the sun in my face?

During the first game I attacked Thad's weak backhand return. "40-0, game." I walked toward the net to change sides, but he called from the baseline, "First good one." Surprised he would take this unfair advantage, I put extra force in my return. He looked foolish trying to reach the shot. Devastating him was going to be easy. Yet he was no fool. Inexperienced players went for force. Thad knew to use spin to destroy an opponent's rhythm. Across the net he chatted away.

After the third game, he reluctantly changed sides. In the fourth game he rushed the net.

I welcomed his serve to my backhand. He had yet to figure out it was my best shot. For variety I tossed in a lob and watched his futile effort to reach the baseline. In four games I lost two points: an unsuccessful drop shot, and a lob he called out. With topspin on the ball, I knew it was good. His cheating only made me determined not to lose another point.

"That's set. 6-0. Stay for one."

He moved off the court and ran a towel over his bare chest. "Come on. I'll get you something to drink."

"Thanks. I would rather play the second set and get going. My baby's with a neighbor."

"Pretty confident, aren't you? I need a drink to cool off."

I thought about leaving. But what would Nell say?

I followed Thad to a redwood deck adjacent to the court where he opened a small refrigerator beneath the bar.

"What'll it be?"

"Just water."

"You've eaten lunch?"

"No. I don't eat before I play."

"I'll make my specialty."

"All I want is water."

"Not very friendly, are you? You wipe me off the court, now refuse my hospitality. Thad's lemonade or nothing."

"Fine...lemonade."

He disappeared into the house. Seated on the shaded porch I felt momentum slipping away. Easier to stay tough across the net. Twenty-six points to win the set. Something nagged when I beat anyone that badly.

Thad returned with two Wilson tennis cans. Until I heard the clinking of ice, I thought he had new balls for the second set. For years, I used an empty tennis can for water. No fancy dispensers at most tournament sites. Wilson, Penn, Dunlop, no matter the brand. The distinct flavor of tennis balls never left the can. Yet this lemonade was thick and sweet like undiluted concentrate and disguised the taste I expected. I took an ice cube in my mouth, careful not to cut my lip on the can's rim. Somewhere I had tasted this odd drink. Thad moved his deck chair closer to mine and we sat there, facing the empty court.

"You're one hell of a player. Seems a shame you gave it up. But you and Nell are on the come-back trail."

"That's a joke."

"A joke? Nell said you won a big doubles tournament in San Francisco last month. Upset the top seeds."

"She and I ended up teaching school in Napa. Our friendship reactivated old dreams of tennis fame."

Thad said nothing, as if he had not heard me.

"Our fathers saw us as champions like little Mo. They didn't foresee accidents. Anyway, I return to the high school soon. I've been on maternity leave this year."

"I thought you and Nell wanted a court to practice on."

"We do, but...."

"But you're quitting."

"Not quitting. Priorities. Husband, baby, school, the full catastrophe," I said, laughing loudly.

"You should stick to tennis. You don't make much teaching, do you? Look at this," Thad said, and stood. "Same weight since I was twenty-five. Know how I keep in shape? Three sets a day, plus an hour with the ball machine. Muscle turns to flab."

"There's other exercise besides tennis. I like to run."

"Races?"

"No...miles on the track."

"What's that prove?"

I took several gulps from the can. "May I have more ice?"

"So... you're a runner now," he said, opening the small refrigerator.

"I don't think you...."

"Hey, give me a break," he said, dumping ice into my can and sitting back down. "What's your weakness? How'd you get beat in tournaments?"

I took a long swallow of lemonade. "Who beat me? Not the good players. But I could lose to dinkers."

"Dinkers?"

"You know. Cheap shots, no form, any means to win."

"You think I'm a dinker?"

"No, dinkers get the ball back."

I saw from his narrowed blue eyes the comment stung.

"What else do you do, besides run around a track?"

An image of Gordon took the edge off a snide reply.

"This summer I've been watching Watergate. An old friend from college was questioned this morning. Conspirators from USC... guys like Donald Segretti. I understand their involvement. Not Gordon's?"

"They're damn fools."

"Gordon isn't a fool. Naïve, and..."

"Mistakes were made."

"Mistakes were made! Are you kidding? Nefarious persons did a lot more than make mistakes. Don't you love the press secretary's use of categorical imperative? Twenty-one letters for the word lie. I don't know if Nixon plays tennis. But he's the quintessential hacker."

"I can do with less political chat and more play. You ready?"

"That's funny. You chatter while you play?"

"Not this set."

I set the empty can beside the deck chair, stood, and grabbed for the chair's flimsy arm.

"I feel dizzy, Thad. Let's finish another day."

From the stairs, he turned and faced me. "You want to use my court? Your girlfriend had a dental appointment and skipped out after a set. You're not doing the same."

He headed to the shady side with the balls.

After the covered deck's shade, the sun felt brutal. Thad's slow serve hovered in the stifling air. A looseness in my arm surprised me, as if I had been soaking in his black-bottomed pool. My backhand went long. I returned the next serve. Thad hit a moon ball back, then another, until my fourth shot went in the net.

I walked slowly to the back fence to get the ball and thought of Sam Erwin's words to Gordon. The senator's wrinkled face reminded me of a southern bulldog. He had drawled, "Young man, what would you tell other young people…interested in a political career in Washington?"

"I would tell them not to come, Sir."

Gordon's voice gripped me again, as it had that morning. My throat tightened. I tried to swallow. My tongue felt coated. No water dispenser on the court. Across the net, Thad looked far away.

"I've got two," he shouted. "You ready?"

"No!"

I lifted my tennis dress and wiped my face. Thad was going to dink me to death. In the first set his ego had put pace on the ball. Now with each shot, he added more spin, making me run for drop shots and lobs that took forever to bounce.

I lost the first game at love.

"Your serve," he yelled.

Even if my timing was off, serving required only athletic faith. All those years with two balls in my hand, a wood racket flat on the court in front of my left foot, the toe of my tennis shoe against the racket's throat. I had learned to toss a ball for the serve this way. Hour after hour of lifting the ball into the air, hoping the ball would land in the center of the racket at my foot. A perfect toss and a perfected swing meant the ball and racket met at the right moment. It was an illusion of connectedness, a Zen moment. The same belief gained long ago from hitting Father's targets.

I served wide and sent Thad into the alley. Moving in, I hit his weak return to the backhand corner for a shot he could not reach. "Fifteen-love." I sent a hard, flat serve to his backhand. "Out," he called. I picked my spot and served the second ball down the middle for what I knew was an ace.

"Double fault," he shouted. Then pointing to his shoes, he turned around.

I knew the game being played. A bad call to foment anger. Then a stall. Thad was going to take extra long to tie his shoelaces. I stared at his backside. His good shape meant he had bent without kneeling. Dizzy as I felt, I trusted my right arm's conditioned memory. Everything in life had been preparation for this moment of freedom. One shot, one bull's eye, and past dreams of fame would no longer adhere.

I dropped the ball, it bounced back up. Then, like a glutinous arrow, the ball flew to its target and nailed Thad in the ass. He whirled. From the look on his face, I was lucky to have a choice of exits. I grabbed my second racket, sailed through the side gate, and never looked back.

Yet I heard his explosive expletive. "You damn bitch."

It was only later, after the summer of Watergate, when the whole sticky political mess unwound and Nixon resigned the Presidency, that I heard Thad's farewell as language befitting the secret White House tapes.

Now it is 2021. A much less intelligent but more rapacious president has left the White House. In these surreal times, I remind myself daily of two truths. When it comes to character, integrity lives and breathes in the individual, or it does not live at all. And regardless of the game being played, a cheater is still a cheater; and lie will always be a three-letter word.

Five Uneasy Pieces

I. To Quit or Not

"The Summer of Watergate" is true except for Thad's name and the shot that nailed him in the ass. The truth is he was going to dink me to death under that intense afternoon sun. I picked up my second racquet and left. Good-bye to his velvet blue court and my delusional return to competitive tennis. At the time I was on leave from teaching high school English. I also for years taught tennis on private courts throughout the Napa Valley and had been the teaching pro at clubs in St. Helena and Napa.

Yet following the birth of a second daughter in late 1976, a fog moves in, such as often occurred in early morning in Napa, and tennis recedes from memory. From 1979 to 1983, living first in Montgomery, Alabama, then three years in a small West German village, the times I played tennis could be counted on one hand. Back in Northern California from 1983 to 1985, I gave lessons at Travis AFB but did not play regularly. Then in the late summer of 1985 we returned to Montgomery where Mike was again a student at Air University. This time we lived on base so our daughters could attend the DODD elementary school. One day that September at the Air University gym, I saw a large poster: *Seven Signs of the Aging Body*. I had two of the seven: heel spurs, and a frozen left shoulder. And because I stupidly thought the shoulder would repair itself, I waited a long time to do anything about it. The USAF physical therapist chided me that this had made his work harder and much longer.

Just now on January 9th, 2023, I stopped "keying" and placed my right hand behind my head, just below my neck. Then I put my left hand behind my back and moved it up as far as I could reach. Next, I intertwined the fingers of both hands and held the position, with my right elbow extended above my head. Why am I telling the reader this? Because when I went to PT the fall of 1985, I could not reach behind to slip my left arm into a coat. I was 42 years old. Luckily, after shoulder restoration, the two C's (chance and circumstance) returned. A military spouse at Maxwell AFB was a certified USLTA tennis instructor and gave lessons on base. Kay and I began hitting regularly and taught clinics together.

The following year, the Air Force sent Mike to the D.C. area for Foreign Service language training. His next posting was Malaysia as Air Attache. We rented a house in Annandale, Virginia. The rental property was part of a community with a pool and two tennis courts. That is when I bought a new racquet, a composite Wilson. This was fortuitous, as Malaysia from 1987 to 1990 is where I again became a tennis player. My delight was to play on grass, which I would have done on the Pacific Northwest tour to Canada in 1960.

Mike's new position was in the DAO office at the U.S. Embassy in Kuala Lumpur (KL). The building was a beautiful new one, with an excellent red & green hardcourt. Once again it was luck that a State Department spouse was an excellent player and had competed in the Fed Cup in Hong Kong when her husband was stationed there before Malaysia. I began practicing regularly with Nancy and played doubles with her in tournaments. Another stroke of good fortune was that Mike's position allowed membership in two private clubs, the Royal Selangor, known as the King's club, with grass and hardcourts, and a second newer club with indoor and outdoor courts. For that club I played on a women's team, comprised of four Japanese women, one Chinese-Malay, and spokeswoman Gail, appointed by the Japanese to speak up because they felt they could not. Once they literally lined up behind me as I delivered their message that we were not playing on wet courts on the top of the KL Hilton and needed to reschedule the match. When we played outdoors some of the Japanese women wore white gloves and such broad hats that they served the way I had in volleyball as a kid. Sideways and shoulder height. They wanted always to play on the indoor courts at our club to avoid exposure to the sun. They found my freckles repellent but loved that I could play three-fourth of the court and lead the team to victory.

Besides my full-time position as an English instructor for Indiana University's Malaysian program, I taught tennis at the U.S. Embassy. First to men and women from the USA, and eventually to Foreign Service Nationals, as local employees were (and are) called. In Malaysia tennis was largely the domain of the wealthy and privileged. In time I became aware that many FSN's had looked at the tennis court with longing after the new embassy's inauguration.

One day while teaching a lesson to a group of spouses, the

Malay who ran the embassy's post office asked me if I would teach a group of FSN's. I said it would be my pleasure and gave him the price for a series of six lessons: thirty ringgit (roughly ten dollars) and a can of new tennis balls. I assumed he would know that I meant per person. He arrived with a large group of employees and exactly what I had told him. I remember laughing, then said I would give them the first series for this amount but negotiate the next round as to payment. This caused consternation because I charged FSN's a small amount compared to my usual fee for a series of lessons. These students began playing tennis among themselves; and given their early arrival at the Embassy, one of them would sign up (it had to be done daily) and reserve the court for after work. This also caused some problems with U.S. embassy employees. When it came time for our family to leave KL, the FSN's organized the Kenna Family Tennis Tournament. The photo from that day delights me (see back cover).

Another pleasure during the Malaysian years was hitting weekly with the Turkish ambassador at the Raintree Club, located close to our residence. Yalcin took his tennis seriously and wanted me to run him all over the court for an hour, non-stop. We hit on an indoor court, while his bodyguard walked around above us with a combat rifle on his shoulder. Yalcin's black Mercedes sat low to the ground, which meant it was armored. When I first met him, I questioned his vehicle and armed bodyguard. He asked me to name the embassy in the world with the most murdered diplomats? "Must be Turkey," I said. "Why?" he asked. I made the semi-shrug of an ignorant American. "The Armenians and the Cypriots like to kill us," he said.

Today I see photos of this retired diplomat on Facebook and marvel that he does not look older than when he and I practiced tennis in the late 1980s. In Malaysia, Yalcin knew George from the U.S. embassy. A Ukrainian by birth, George worked for the Agency. He was an avid golfer, tennis player, and spy. I had the unique experience of accompanying George to several embassies in Kuala Lumper. Why? George had made a repeated challenge that he and a female could beat any embassy's best male tennis team. The climax to this challenge was our second match against the French, days before George and his family left Malaysia. I tell this story at the end of *Tennis Talk of a Nobody.*

In August of 1990, our family left Malaysia. A difficult departure for daughters Michelle & Bonnie, and Mike. For me leaving Malaysia felt beyond painful. I had loved teaching three years for Indiana University. I relished live-in help, a brilliant amah who when we left, became the cook at the U.S. ambassador's residence. From August 1990 until January 2022, Luan stayed in her position, as U.S. ambassadors came and went.

If I departed Malaysia with a heavy heart, I also left with a healthy, toned body. And I vowed not to quit tennis again.

Back in the D.C. area that August of 1990, we rented the same house in Annandale. Then another stroke of luck. Nancy, my tennis friend from Malaysia, was living in Northern Virginia, and that year she and I met in Reston each Saturday to practice. Otherwise, life consisted of studying at the Foreign Service Institute in Arlington: six hours of Spanish five days a week, two hours in the car, and several hours of study at night. I think of that year and see a family of four seated at the kitchen table with schoolbooks in front of them. Sitting is what I never wanted to do in life, unless I was reading or writing; and as a teacher, I usually stood and moved around in classrooms. Yet during those 32 weeks of Spanish, I told myself that Venezuela offered a perfect climate for playing a lot of tennis, as I had in Malaysia.

Five years earlier at Maxwell AFB, I had written an article for the *Air Force Times*. The piece purported to be about tennis but was about language & sexism in the military. But be assured that no male tennis player at Air University took my side of the court! It took moving to Caracas, Venezuela, to encounter *machismo*.

In late August of 1991, close to our residence in *Prados del Este,* I located a public tennis facility and hired a man no taller than I, to hit with me twice a week. He called himself a pro and did have baskets of tennis balls. I thought this would help me get back in shape, and so I jogged from home to the courts, and back again. After a few weeks, this fellow told me he was organizing a mixed-doubles tournament and wanted me to play with one of his students. Forget 32 weeks of Spanish, as nothing at the Foreign Service Institute prepared me to understand Spanish in Caracas where endings of words were eaten, such as 'ma o men' for 'mas o menos'. Which is to say I lacked a way to explain why I did not want to play, and this diminutive 'pro' went ahead and signed me up. My partner, a good-looking man in his early fifties had fancy equipment & attire but no game to match them. We won in the first round because I dominated the court and relegated him to the alley. As everyone shook hands, I understood him to say *la gringa* had won the match. The term

Life in the Times

LADIES
WOMEN

ON THE HOMEFRONT
By Gail Kenna
'Girl'-hood must end sometime

Something's been bugging me for a long time, but yesterday when the men and the "girls" played round robin mixed doubles, my irritation came to the fore. The "girls" were married to senior officers, a fact that provides a clue to their ages.

I know it's considered poor taste to discuss a woman's age or to seek such information over a casual game of tennis, but I'm certain not one of yesterday's girls was young. Even though I can't specify ages, I did note they had those telltale signs of age one sees so vividly on a warm sunny day: blotches of red fish-purple veins, bulging thighs, and, god forbid, cellulite.

I know for a fact that during the tail end of my girlhood, say around the age of 12, I had firm legs without a trace of broken blood vessels or cellulite. But my girlhood went the way of the horseless carriage, so why am I still labeled a girl today?

I'm well aware the feminists stewed over this issue of girl vs. woman eons ago, but apparently their message didn't permeate the military social mileau. In the squadron my husband commanded, he always referred to the men and the women of the 60th OMS, not the men and the girls. Yet in a military social setting, I rarely hear "woman" spoken, while usage of girl, lady and spouse abounds.

My Webster's 20th century unabridged dictionary tells me, in definition four, that "a girl can be a woman of any age, married or single." That's exactly the kind of ambiguity that drives me mad. It's insulting, if not downright absurd, to suggest I can be called at age 80 what I was called at age 8. I don't think men face the same problem with "boy." My Webster's allows that a boy can mean any man or fellow, but if someone tells me he hired a new boy to do the lawn, I assume the worker is young.

But if the use of "girl" confines women to one phase in life (a dependent one, I might add) then "lady" imposes a role from bygone days and conjures images of idle Victorian women gazing through lace curtains at life on the street. My slang dictionary, unlike Webster's, offers a plethora of meanings for lady and reveals just how demeaning the word can be. Webster tells us "lady" means a woman of good breeding or some social position, the correlative to gentleman. Yet the correlatives aren't always evident.

Of course, lots of people regard arguments over word usage as a waste of time. But recently I was struck by the absurdity of not looking closely at how we use words. I received a letter written to military wives in which women were addressed repeatedly as ladies and told what the girls were doing, but also asked to consider various positions as chairperson. The whole purpose of chairperson, obnoxious sounding word that it is, had to do with sexist language. How, I wondered, can the girls and the ladies be signing up to be chairpersons?

But enough said. It's time to dash to a shopping mall and locate a store that imprints T-shirts. The men and the girls are playing mixed doubles again in two weeks, and I have it in mind to wear a shirt that says, "Your partner is a woman." If nothing else, getting the identities straight might help me regain my half of the court.

Gail Kenna is a free-lance writer from Maxwell AFB, Ala.

An article I wrote in 1986 for the standing column, "On the Homefront," which appeared in The Air Force Times *– a monthly publication for Air Force members and their famlies..*

was pejorative in Venezuela. I should not have been surprised in our next match that afternoon, which his wife and adult son came to watch. My partner morphed into a maniac! He went for everything at net or ran behind his weak serve into 'no man's land' and was easy pickings for the other team. The balls served to him, he slammed, with most of them going out or hitting the back fence. The opponents shook their heads. His wife and son looked mortified. Never in my years of playing tennis had I seen what I experienced that day. Obviously, the other players hit only to my partner except when they served to me. We lost my serve because this macho male ran for any shot that crossed the net. That day was the only time I have refused to shake hands at the end of a match. I shook the other team's hands and would not take his. His son, a young man, caught up with me as I was leaving the tennis complex. In English he apologized for his father's behavior of preferring to lose instead of letting me win the match for them. Perhaps there was hope for this younger generation of men?

After school began for Michelle and Bonnie, we hired a driver to take them to and from the International School. This young man, Luis, drove me wherever I needed to go in Caracas, a ten-mile basin with five million inhabitants and horrendous traffic. That first year, Mike was given membership in a prestigious golf club in Caracas. It had excellent tennis courts, and the professional was a welcome contrast to the unpolished pro in *Prados del Este*. I began taking weekly lessons. Soon the pro asked me to play on the club's team, which needed a good singles player. Once again, I acquiesced. Why? Whenever

I ventured out in Caracas, I felt tongue-tied. Words, always a loving companion, abandoned me in a second language until I pushed through a language barrier and spoke my FSI Spanish. Until then I was a deaf mute.

The day of the first match at the country club, I wore long white cotton pants from the Malaysian days, a polo shirt, and not the cleanest of tennis shoes. My opponent from another club was already on the grandstand court in smart apparel, with two matching racquets. It took only a few balls to realize she was woefully inexperienced. Her husband was there and kept talking to her, as he walked back and forth outside the court.

That Saturday in Caracas I relived a tournament in Northern California from the mid 1970s. My opponent in Stockton in a first-round match had new equipment and spiffy attire. Her husband and two children were with her, seated on a bench behind the fenced court. In the first game, I served three aces. She hit my other serve in the net. I won the next game at love and watched her anguished gestures to her family. She raised both hands with open palms, as if to ask, *what can I do?* Nothing. In the first set, she won two points. One ball she hit dribbled over the net, and I double-faulted once. This meant I won the first set in 26 points. She came to the net and said she should not have entered the tournament and was defaulting. As I shook her hand, the misery and embarrassment in her face imprinted. I recalled it that day in Caracas and hoped this woman would quit after the first set. But the husband kept shouting at his wife, telling her how to play me, as if she could manufacture the drop shot or lob or slice that he commanded her to hit. I won easily, left the club, and did not return. *Adios, el tenis.* I ripped that poster of the aging body out of my mind. But my decision to quit tennis a third time was sealed in a strange way.

I had been hired to teach for Shelton State, an Alabama community college, which had an evening program at the school our daughters attended. My students were high school graduates, mostly Venezuelans, or sons and daughters of diplomats, and most of them wanted to study in the United States. I taught the basic English composition courses, 101 and 102, and literature electives. That first year, a young male Venezuelan took English 101. He had returned recently to Caracas from Florida, where he had been a tennis student at the famous Bollettier Academy in Bradenton. Rob (U.S. nickname) had been a top-ranked player in Venezuela and gone to Florida hopeful about his future as a tennis champion. He returned defeated. His parents spent a fortune and his education had been poor. His written English was not at a level for U.S. colleges, his written Spanish inadequate for Venezuelan universities, and he no longer wanted to play tennis. Once I knew his story, I told him he could use the class to write about his experience in Florida. This adolescent player had arrived there with confidence, was looked at the first week, then the famous *maestro* made his selection. This Venezuelan and many others were assigned to the back courts. Yes, they played a lot of tennis, took high school classes, fooled around as youth will. But Rob realized he was not going to be playing on tour ever and returned home. It was through conversations with him and reading his essays that I admitted something to myself about defeat and why I kept quitting tennis. Did I resolve to face this conflict in myself? No. Instead, I went to prison.

And the Venezuelan prisons I visited had lots of cement but no tennis courts. Yet they held incarcerated North Americans and I spent four years helping them. This is all recounted in *Beyond the Wall*, which won a grant from the Puffin Foundation of New Jersey in 2000 and was reprinted in 2021. In Caracas I also worked with charities, which the U.S. Embassy helped to support: a home for unwed mothers, one for pensioners, another for orphaned and abandoned boys where I taught English. I wrote an epistolary novel, *Face of the Avila*, with a journalist from New York, as our way to explore Venezuelan culture and the difficulties it presented, especially to newcomers. Daughter Michelle had been in Caracas only half of her senior year and following the first *golpe de estado* in early 1992, she returned to Annandale to complete high school. Bonnie spent all four years of high school in Caracas. Both she and I, as the plane took off that August day in 1995, had tears in our eyes. Not Mike, who after four years as the Defense Attache felt relief and looked ahead to his new position as Dean of the Attache school at Bolling AFB.

From 1992 until the late spring of 1997, I did not pick up a racquet. Back in the D.C. area I sought full-time work and was hired at American University. After that first year of teaching and in terrible shape, I felt an urge to play tennis again. The sport had gotten me back in condition before. Mike played golf at the Army-Navy club in Arlington, and one Saturday in late May I went with him to use the tennis backboard there. The club's assistant pro came over and after watching me, asked if I would play with a new female member, a retired Air Force one-star general. I told the pro my husband was Air Force and to please give this woman my name and telephone number. Soon she called me. But after we played the first time, I was unable to walk up and down the stairs of our three-story townhouse, except sideways and by taking one stairstep at a time. That June of 1997, I was scheduled to visit daughter Michelle in Germany at her first army posting, then to fly to London for a three-week writing course at Merton College, Oxford. I hobbled all that time and even after I returned home. Mike had seen and liked an orthopedic at Bolling AFB and made an appointment for me. The day of Mike's retirement ceremony in September at Bolling, I saw the orthopedic that afternoon. The receptionist said I was lucky to get to see a god. I was not sure what to make of this, though Mike had raved about the orthopedic. I told the doctor I had injured my left knee and added, "Maybe it's just age." (I was 54.) I heard words I would not forget.

"Cut the old age shit." He pointed to the hallway and told me to walk up and down slowly, then again rapidly. He stood outside the doorway and watched. "Nothing wrong with your gait," he said. We went back into the office. He asked what I had been doing the past year? I told him about teaching at AU, sitting to teach, grade papers, prepare lessons, and then had played tennis one day after a five-year layoff.

"Well, what did you expect? Your legs are out of shape. Get on a bike. Start playing tennis again. Or hang it up." He ended by telling me he could take a man of eighty and build him up. I have not made this handsome young doctor sound charming, which he was. On the way out, I smiled at the receptionist. But I did not say a god had spoken and I would follow his commandment.

A friend from our time in Germany, a retired three-star USAF general, William Earl Brown, convinced me to join Northern Virginia's Golden Racquets for players 55 and over. This group was great because I ran all over the court while older male players stayed at the net to avoid running. At one point I did ask Mike to buy me a wedding band. Mike as a USAF pilot had not worn a wedding ring, so I had not worn one. It turned out that several members of the Golden Racquets were widowed and sought a "younger" wife. I kept being asked out. I still wear the gold band that Mike gave me. During 1998 he worked for the State Department in Bogotá. I stayed in Falls Church until after daughter Michelle's wedding in June of 1999, then returned to Colombia with Mike.

As it turned out, his apartment in Bogotá was not far from the U.S. ambassador's residence on a hill. At the high point of the property was a beautiful, perfectly maintained red clay court. Even better was the cement wall at one end. The entire width of the court was a backboard, with a net line painted on the smooth wall. I could not believe my luck. I had only to walk several streets, show my carnet to the guards, and go up to the court. Our apartment was on a busy street. We did not use the patio because it stayed filthy from the unleaded gas in Colombia. And what was there to see except traffic? But at the ambassador's court and just below it, I could sit in a chair by a fishpond with the finest view of Bogotá. I could stay there for hours if I wanted, running from one end of the backboard to the other, practicing ground strokes, volleys, and serves. I had joined a gym in July of 1999, one in an old Spanish house, a charming place to work out and ride an exercise bike. Between the gym and the red clay court, I loved being in Bogotá, and its 8000 feet elevation improved my stamina. At the time I was awarded a grant to write a book about the four years in Caracas with imprisoned North Americans. Writing meant sitting, and tennis I knew could offset this. No quitting the sport again.

During the years in Bogotá from June 1999 until January of 2002, I paid two different Colombians to hit with me. The second one, Jose, played in tournaments, had taken clinics from visiting professionals, and was a strong player. In 2001 he taught the female U.S. ambassador in the early morning before I arrived for practice. Jose spoke only Spanish, but in Bogotá that meant Castilian, the Spanish I had learned at FSI in Arlington.

One morning Jose's face showed worry. He thought he had insulted the ambassador. Jose told me he had taken a clinic in Bogotá with a pro from Miami, who kept yelling, "Move your ass." Jose had said this to the ambassador that morning and received a shocked look. *Qué sentido?* he asked. (What meaning?) I turned around and placed a hand on each cheek. *Culo,* Jose. He did not laugh but asked if he should return tomorrow. *Absolutamente!* I said the ambassador was paying him to get her running and might take what he said to heart!

And my heart? I left Bogotá with sadness. I had taught English courses to U.S. Marines at the embassy, completed *Beyond the Wall,* loved walking in Bogotá with its high altitude, met gracious people, spoke Castilian Spanish, and felt strong again on a tennis court. Mike and I had time together and although travel was restricted, we managed trips related to his work, such as to Cartagena. Our daughters had visited us in Bogotá, as had friends. Then news came in early 2002 and Mike was being assigned to the U.S. Embassy in Peru.

Sea level Lima, half a year of a strange fog, a disappointing apartment after the two in Bogotá. Across from the long wall of glass that comprised our fifth-floor apartment was Lima's country club for the rich. With envy Mike looked at the golf course and I at the red & green hardcourts. No hope of playing there. But I was not quitting tennis again. I ended up walking several days a week to the Lima tennis center with its dry clay courts. The tennis center had eager ball boys hanging around. Most played tennis so it was easy to hire one to hit and another to collect balls. The desperation in their lives tugged at me emotionally each time I went there. I collected used clothes and racquets for them. What else could I do? The dust affected my eyes, and my knees began to bother me in a way they had not in Bogotá's high altitude. Oh, woe is me. Then a phone call to get to North Carolina immediately to care for two-year-old Lauryn while Michelle and Pat were in the Middle East for the second Gulf war. "I am not quitting tennis," I reminded myself, packing a duffle bag with dozens of practice balls. Then off to Miami, onto Raleigh in the winter of 2003. I took Lauryn to childcare for several hours each weekday, then hit balls on a backboard or used a court to practice serves until the library opened at 11:00, wrote and read for several hours, and returned in mid-afternoon to the childcare center. Just a grandmother and a two-year-old, in a tiny house in Sanford. But I had not quit tennis, just made it a solo sport for those months until Michelle and Pat returned from the war.

In October of 2004, Mike and I left Lima and moved to the Northern Neck of Virginia where we had bought land in 1998. We assumed there were tennis courts in the area but discovered no public or high school courts in Northumberland and Lancaster counties. But there was Indian Creek, a private club with an indoor tennis facility. Indoor, another of the two C's! And for over seventeen years I have loved the pleasure of playing with no sun to worry about and no hat on my head. I have been able to play in all weather and at any hour of the day and night. A wonderful woman named Pat was the professional here for decades until George, another excellent tennis professional, took over as the club's pro. At almost eighty I play tennis each week with four different men (all younger) and hit another day to help a good friend with her game. In completing *Tennis Talk of a Nobody* I have explored what I had not understood about tennis in my life. An example would be during the U.S. Open in September 2022.

I, along with four million television viewers, watched the final match in the long career of Serena Williams. I first heard about Venus back in Malaysia when the journalist James Fallows occasionly played tennis with me at the embassy. One day he told me about a new California tennis star who had played her first professional match in Oakland, California. This memory makes me aware of how long the Williams sisters have been around: both competing and winning for more than three decades. Beauty in motion, no. But grit, determination, and lethal serves, yes.

At the time of Serena's announced retirement, I read an article in the *Wall Street Journal* about a player named Ann Miller. She had beaten Williams when Serena debuted in Toronto in 1993. Serena won only one game from Ann, whose highest world ranking was forty. The WSJ reporter located Ann Miller Boras in Oregon, a married woman with two children, and interviewed her about the Serena match. What stuck me was that Ann quit tennis at 23. She talked about the "grind of professional tennis." At the time of the reporter's call, she had joined a mixed-doubles league and run into problems with the USLTA. They still had her as a ranked professional player, and she wanted to play in a regular league. Whether 4.5 or 5.0, the article did not say. Decades without tennis is the point, and she admitted to not watching televised tennis.

From the article, I learned that in high school in Michigan, she had left home for the Bollettieri Academy (IMG) in Florida, then joined the women's worldwide tour until she quit tennis. Her story interested me. She admitted to being lonely on tour, but otherwise the article did not state her reason for quitting tennis. One obvious one, at least to me, would be inner conflict. I can only imagine the questions Ann might have asked herself. Who am I playing for? Is this what I want out of life? What does it mean to spend life trying to beat other players? How close can I be to those I compete against? Am I considered a somebody, a champion, only if I reach the top and win a major?

Will sponsors stay with me unless I win some tournaments? Do I love what I am doing, which is devoting my life to tennis?

Reading the WSJ article about Ann Miller Boras made me ask a question which was waiting to be answered all along: *How did tennis outrage my nature?*

II. Outraging My Nature

"We must acknowledge the weakness of our nature"

Rene Descartes, 1596-1650

Yes, we must, and my question is this. Should a dreamy, red-haired child who loved to read, who listened obsessively to "The Green Door" on the radio, who created dramas for her dolls, and whose dream was to take piano lessons, be a competitive tennis player?

Photos from the late 1940s show me at the beach in a bonnet, with a shirt over a two-piece bathing suit. While living in Arizona from age three to seven, my father's work with Sunkist Growers took our family to Southern California during the summer where we rented a cottage at Newport. My dark-haired mother tanned, but I had a recessive gene for red hair from my paternal grandfather Robert and maternal great-grandmother Sara. The same was true for my older brother Barry. Both of us freckled and burned. In Arizona I learned to swim at Tempe's public outdoor pools. And once, when I would not get under an umbrella, my mother taught me a lesson. She let me stay in the water for as long as I wanted. My face and shoulders were so burned she had to use a needle to pop the blisters, which ran and eventually scabbed. "Do you see now what the sun does to you, Gail?" are words I probably heard. Years later, 1953 in Fullerton, California, Mother argued with Father when he said I would be taking tennis lessons. Her words I remember hearing. "Theron, she'll burn herself all up in the sun."

Besides my father's wish for me to play tennis, he had made an important decision in Tempe, Arizona, which altered my life. I had gone to kindergarten at Arizona State's teacher training school. I hated being there and remember the day, running wildly to get away from school, I took a bad spill on the asphalt and ended up with bloody knees and hands. At the time my brother was having trouble reading, given the new sight method used at the "training" school. This was enough to convince my father that I should go to the other elementary school in Tempe, one in an old brick building where Mexican children went. Father had been told the first-grade teacher at the Grammar School taught reading through phonics, and he overrode my mother who wanted me to attend the training school, an *Anglo* enclave.

A photo from first grade shows 34 students, though who knows how many were not there for the class picture. It does appear there was a run on the striped tee shirt in Tempe before photo day. I am in the second row with a big smile. I loved Miss Thieu and first grade. Mother had curled my red hair and made the dress with its row of ruffles. I can in memory easily revisit first grade, especially one day in the music room. We sang a 'round' of "row, row, row your boat." I sensed in one line seven words to remember: "Row your boat/gently down the stream" and kept wondering about its meaning. On another day, Miss Thieu asked me to read to the class. When I finished, she stood in the back and applauded, and asked the students to join in. Her words never left me. "Gail is a reader." With four words she conferred an identify on me. Yes, I was a reader and loved words. And I have Father to thank for his sagacity in making the decision to change me from one school to the other.

On outraging my nature, I will speak first of the outer and visible me.

Flash forward nineteen years to 1968 in San Antonio, Texas. I had married Mike, a USAF student-pilot, moved to Randolph Air Force base, and ended up teaching tennis that summer. At the time I had a suspicious black spot on my lower lip, as if a fly had landed there. One afternoon I went from the tennis courts to a

First grade class, Tempe, Arizona. I'm in the second row, third from the right.

medical appointment. "Why are you dressed that way?" the dermatologist asked. I told him I taught tennis on base and had been a competitive player in Southern California. "You," he said, his finger pointed at me, "should be nowhere near the sun." I made a quip that tennis was the way I expressed myself. He said I ought to express myself indoors, playing

Above and top: *Whether on the beach or in the backyard, from the very beginning I was always bonneted against the sun.*

102

the piano. I remember laughing at these ironic words. Days later I returned for surgery. And staring into a mirror above me, I watched the black spot removed and black stitches sewn into my lower lip. I started teaching at Harlandale High in San Antonio the next week with those stitches, which brought stares from faculty and students. To the latter, four classes of sophomores, I said I had lost the fight.

My USAF medical file from 1968 to 1998 is primarily dermatology appointments. I knew of the sun's danger because my brother in 1965 spent months in the Balboa Naval hospital after removal of a malignant melanoma. His calf of one leg ended up concave with multiple skin grafts; and lymph nodes were taken from his groin to keep the cancer from spreading. He had ignored Mother's warnings about the sun from Arizona onward. I wore a hat when I taught tennis but not when I played matches. And SPF lotions and creams did not develop in any significant commercial way until into the 1970s.

In retrospect, I wish I had kept a journal of encounters with dermatologists. One I have not forgotten is a USAF dermatologist I saw soon after my second daughter Bonnie was born in 1976 at Travis AFB in Northern California. I was thirty-three, felt fat and out of shape. The dermatologist took one look at me and said, "Do you know you have the skin of a 65 year-old woman?" I must have wanted to cry but asked sarcastically, "Does that mean when I'm 65 I'll have the skin of a 95 year-old woman?" I did like the USAF "derm" in Tucson in the mid-90s whose first question was, "Which country in the world has the worst skin cancer rates?" He did not wait for me to think of an answer. "Australia," he said. "English, aren't you? Your forebears were meant for foggy London or Edinburgh, not down under, baking in the Australian sun or here in the Arizona desert."

As it turns out, my English forebears came to the New World and settled in Virginia and Pennsylvania. One ancestor born in 1600 in London, died in 1666 in Northumberland County where I have lived since 2004. Other ancestors headed West in the early 1900s, settling in Southern California, a desert made green with stolen water and meant for the darker skin of early inhabitants: native Indians and Mexicans. In my elementary school days, when Mother and I took a train from Fullerton to Los Angeles, I envied the black porters their skin. Oh, to have dark skin and not freckle and burn, I thought as a child, unaware then of prejudice about skin color.

Earlier I mentioned the four Japanese women who played tennis with me in Kuala Lumpur, Malaysia. The Japanese have a proverb, which says white skin covers flaws; that a fair-skinned woman is beautiful, even if her features are not attractive. I laugh now, remembering what Patricia, a Chinese dressmaker in KL, said the first time she met me. She pointed to my bare arms and said, "What you call those?" "Freckles," I said. "Very ugly. Make long sleeves for you!"

I no longer have a colored chalk drawing of myself at age sixteen. During a tennis tournament in Santa Monica, the daughter of my host family took me to a local fair. At one point that evening, an artist called to me and said if I would sit down and allow him to draw me, I could have a portrait for free. He said people would stop to watch him draw my hazel, deep-set eyes. I agreed to this but asked him to draw me without freckles.

The drawing surprised me, as I liked my face without spots all over it. But more than my skin bothered me. I disliked my hair, its color and natural curl, and being teased about being a redhead. "Hey, freckle face, you belong in a zoo. Hey, red, where's the fire?" That was the playground in the past, before today's "be kind" ethos, which given the divisive climate in our country, strikes me as ironic.

I do sympathize with those who believe they are in the wrong body and would like to change gender. This I never felt, but I begrudged my freckled skin, hair color and height. Or lack of it. In sixth grade I remember the afternoon when each student, one by one in front of the class, was weighed and measured. I was the second tallest in the class, with only a giant of a girl named Mary Beth above me. I was just over five feet and weighed 100 pounds. By eighth grade I was 5'3" and stopped growing. Being this height did not make me eager to rush the net and face top spin lobs. Yet I did not disparage the shape of my body until high school in Health class when I learned I was a mesomorph. I longed to be an ectomorph and have a thin body and long neck like Audrey Hepburn. Instead, I was short-waisted, long-legged for my height, muscular, and had inherited a fat gene, which meant I easily put on pounds. Not getting fat is hard work, Mother would tell me. She kept her figure through diligence. She lived until almost 98, and she often said, "I may be old. But I am not fat." It is widely accepted but ignored by an enlarging population, that as few as five extra pounds is a problem for knees. And my Rumanian tennis coach reminded me that extra pounds slowed me down on the court.

Besides skin that freckled, weight that easily increased, and limited height, I hated my non-white, uneven teeth. Tennis threw me into a world of the monied. And "rich" kids in Fullerton wore braces. Orthodontia work was out of the question on my father's salary. We had a kind elderly dentist who explained I could not brush away naturally yellow teeth, but Dr. Howe said to use baking soda on them. It was this aging and trusted dentist who recognized in the summer of 1963 that I was seriously anemic (pernicious, in fact). That summer during June and July, I had been teaching tennis by day and working at Disneyland at night in the Sunkist Citrus House on Main Street. Sunkist was located between the candy palace and the Carnation ice cream parlor. At night I often traded orange juice for peanut brittle and ice cream. "What has happened to your teeth?" Dr. Howe asked at the beginning of August. He called my mother who worked for Dr. Struve, an internist. The next thing I knew I was in a lab for a blood draw, then told by this doctor to quit both jobs, rest, eat liver and eggs daily; and if the next blood draw at the end of the month showed I still had pernicious anemia, I was not going back to USC for my junior year. He also ordered shots, which were given in my rear and gave me a blackened bum that lasted for a year. Ah, youth. Triple cone of stupidity in my case. Now at 79, I have reached the single scoop stage. Yet when I turn 80 in June, it will be with teeth neither white or straight, but all are mine.

Thus far, what I have talked about is my genetic heritage of skin, body type, height, and teeth. It is the internal *outrage* that concerns me. Why have I used this word and what does it mean? My OED has this definition for outrage: To treat with violence, to violate flagrantly, to injure and arouse deep anger and indignation, to deeply offend. This is not a simple subject, and I will approach it as a teacher.

A memory just came to me of an introductory tennis lesson I gave to youngsters when I taught for the Fullerton Recreation Department in summer during my college years. I modeled the lesson partly on a poem, which I had read my freshman year at USC in English 102, the class for composition and literature. On the following page is the poem, "Naming of Parts" by Henry Reed. In the poem, the instructor uses a gun. My lesson was for a tennis racquet.

I see and hear myself now with a group of elementary-age kids in front of me. I always had to tell them to spread out and make a large enough circle to keep any child's head from getting bashed. Next, I would show them how to hold the racquet out in front of them. I would say, "Run your fingers around the frame of the racquet. What do we call this? The head. And inside the head is a network of crisscrossed strings. If in our lessons I say to lower your head, I do not mean the one above your shoulders. But no surprise that under the head of your racquet is the throat." (Wood racquets had narrow throats. Now they are wide and hollow.) After the throat I continued to the last part. "At the bottom of the racquet is the grip. And what do you need? A firm grip on the grip, to keep the head from wobbling when the ball hits your racquet. Remember to apply pressure with your third, second, and first fingers, and you must keep your thumb around the grip. Just three parts to remember: the head, the throat, the grip."

Naming of Parts
by Henry Reed, 1942

Today we have naming of parts. Yesterday,
We had daily cleaning. And tomorrow morning,
We shall have what to do after firing. But to-day,
Today we have naming of parts. Japonica
Glistens like coral in all of the neighbouring gardens,
And today we have naming of parts.
This is the lower sling swivel. And this
Is the upper sling swivel, whose use you will see,
When you are given your slings. And this is the piling swivel,
Which in your case you have not got. The branches
Hold in the gardens their silent, eloquent gestures,
Which in our case we have not got.
This is the safety-catch, which is always released
With an easy flick of the thumb. And please do not let me
See anyone using his finger. You can do it quite easy
If you have any strength in your thumb. The blossoms
Are fragile and motionless, never letting anyone see
Any of them using their finger.
And this you can see is the bolt. The purpose of this
Is to open the breech, as you see. We can slide it
Rapidly backwards and forwards: we call this
Easing the spring. And rapidly backwards and forwards
The early bees are assaulting and fumbling the flowers:
They call it easing the Spring.
They call it easing the Spring: it is perfectly easy
If you have any strength in your thumb: like the bolt,
And the breech, and the cocking-piece, and the point of balance,
Which in our case we have not got; and the almond-blossom
Silent in all of the gardens and the bees going backwards and forwards,
For today we have naming of parts.

Following my June USC graduation in 1965, I taught tennis that summer before leaving for San Francisco State and graduate school. After earning a secondary teaching credential, I returned to Southern California in early 1967. One day in a three-year junior high, I used "Naming of Parts" with a class of eighth graders. It was my first semester of paid teaching in the Los Angeles school district. Given the turbulent times and the Vietnam War, plus a curriculum that mandated lessons on figurative language, I thought Henry Reed's poem would be a good choice for a lesson. Most of my students were from Wilmington and San Pedro, bused to a white school near Palos Verdes. One student I remember well was Anna, an Italian girl, whose father worked as a longshoreman. I would have noted this for two reasons. A man new to the faculty at Dodson Junior high had become a history teacher in middle age. But Domenic, who became my friend, continued to work as a longshoreman on weekends and during the summer. My father spent time at the docks in and around Long Beach, dealing with shipping companies that exported Sunkist citrus. His work involved negotiations with the longshoreman's union in Los Angeles and San Francisco. This is background as to why Anna's life had special resonance for me.

After I read the poem aloud in class (each student had a copy), Anna asked, "What kind of man talks that way?" She meant the voice at the end of each stanza. I probably said, "A poetic and sensitive man. Someone who loves nature and must go off to fight a war." Anna was a bright girl and not afraid to ask questions. Weeks later she came to my room during the lunch hour and asked if "obnoxious" was a dirty word. "No," I told her, and asked why she would think this about a word I used often with unruly "bus" boys, telling them to stop being obnoxious. Anna told me she had called her little brother "obnoxious" while her family ate dinner and her father slapped her. I remember thinking, as I would through a long career of teaching, how a moment such as this was meant to remind me of how little I knew about the lives of my students.

As I recalled this incident just now, I thought of the 1954 movie, *On the Waterfront*, set in a world of mob bosses and dock workers. I can imagine Anna's father as one of those toughened men, slapping his daughter because she used a word he did not know, and of Anna as hearing men speak the way her father did. I have seen *On the Waterfront* many times. In memory I hear Marlo Brando as Terry Malloy tell his brother Charley, "I could have been somebody, instead of a nobody, which is what I am." Terry had been a boxer, and his brother had fixed a fight, which Terry had to lose for the big boss, Mr. Friendly. America, America, land of winners and losers. Yet in the end, Terry stands up for what is right and just on the waterfront. At age eleven and in years to follow, this film spoke powerfully to me about fighting injustice.

If the reader is wondering what the connections are in my mind, which combine the Henry Reed poem, a lesson on a tennis racquet, and a classroom with Anna, I can only say these are woven and connected within the frame of my past. What if it is not in a child's nature to compete, to want to win above all else? Can such an urge and behavior be drilled into a child or adolescent? Does a necessary rebellion occur from outraging the basic nature in ourselves? Best not to join the U.S. Marine Corps, or engage in one-on-one, win or lose combat on a tennis court with a nature like the sensitive recruit. In the poem he has no choice about learning to use a gun and carry it off to war. Yet he exercised the freedom in his mind and sought beauty beyond the naming of parts. Which is why I found meaning in this poem from the first time I read it and why I used it in teaching.

What I loved on a tennis court was teaching the sport and later in a classroom, teaching language and literature. In third grade, my teacher Miss Leander had me help those whose reading was falling behind. Most were boys and the one I remember most was Fred, a special friend throughout my school years in Fullerton. Miss Leander told me one day that I was meant to be a teacher. She gave me an identity the way Miss Thieu had when she called me a reader. My point is that competition and being focused to beat opponents violated something within me. Several vignettes come to mind as a way I might show this. One relates to the successful tennis player, Darlene Hard, and the second to a 1958 gold runner-up trophy from Ojai, California.

III. Remembering Darlene Hard

Once again, the two C's: chance and circumstance. How else to explain that on December 2nd, 2022, I decided to research Darlene Hard on the internet. This Grand Slam champion and fellow Californian had handed me a trophy in March of 1958 in Fullerton. In 1957 she had won the Wimbledon doubles with Althea Gibson but lost the singles championship to Althea that year. I would have known about this in 1958 because of local news that Hard would play in the annual adult and youth tournament in Fullerton.

What mystified me on December 2, 2022, was to learn that on that same day one year earlier, December 2, 2021, Hard died in Southern California. An obituary by Richard Evans in *The Guardian* related something that surprised me. Hard had worked at USC, my alma mater, for *The Daily Trojan*, the campus newspaper, from 1981 to 2016. He noted something else for his

U.K. audience, which I knew nothing about. "Either by design or just because the gesture fitted her generous personality, the blonde Californian planted a big kiss on Gibson's cheek at the 1957 Centre Court presentation ceremony." Evans went on to say, "In the 1950s the kiss made quite a statement." He meant racially, given that Gibson, despite her many wins at Wimbledon, was never allowed to be a member of the Queen's Lawn Tennis Association. From the obituary, I learned that Hard won 21 Grand Slam titles: 3 in singles, 13 in doubles, and 5 in mixed. Yet in her 35 years at USC, Darlene's tennis fame was unknown to those she worked with at USC's student newspaper. One exception, according to Richard Evans, was Roy Emerson's daughter. She knew about Hard because her father, the famous Australian tennis player, had been Darlene's partner for mixed-doubles victories.

I mention Darleen Hard and the trophy she handed me because of the final I played that day in 1958. Would I have been nervous that this Grand Slam winner was there? Possibly. A good-sized crowd assembled to watch the finals in Girl's Fifteen and under. I was playing Sally, someone I liked. In my years of playing competitive tennis, I never figured out how to compete against someone I considered a friend. Yet I found it easy to be tough against players I disliked, especially those who were dishonest when it came to tennis ethics.

The summer before this match, it so happened Sally was in Newport Beach at the same time as my family's annual two-week vacation. That summer Father was recovering from a ruptured appendix that almost caused his death. One June evening Sally and I sat on the low wall in front of our cottage, and I listened to her talk about problems in her family. As I remember the conversation, her older sister had played tennis and done well, then suddenly quit. Sally was the one to take her place. But she expressed ambivalence about this, felt pressure from her father, said she had other interests and was conflicted because of starting high school in the fall, as was I.

Our match that March went to three sets, and I lost. After Sally and I shook hands, my father asked what had happened to me. He said I had played ball after ball from the baseline, balls

GIRLS' TROPHY WINNERS — Darlene Hard (R) gives Sally Raymond first place trophy and congratulations for her win over Gail Wilson. (L) in the Girls' Singles of the Fullerton Invitational Tennis Tournament. Hard is top-seeded in the Women's Open division. (News Tribune Photo)

that were clearly out. Some of those in the audience had asked him what was wrong with me. Did I need glasses? He did not mean the occasional ball. He said this happened throughout the third set, as if I did not want to win the match.

When I think of the 1950s, I think of silence, a world of the unspoken beneath a surface hiding societal problems. Which is to say I would not have spoken aloud of the dilemma I felt that day, or of so much that bothered me in adolescence and the 1950s. How to explain that I had not wanted to beat Sally? I thought of her as a friend and felt the first-place trophy might encourage her to keep playing so she would not quit tennis.

Yet when I played doubles, my deepest need was to not let down my partner, which meant it did not matter who was on the other side of the net. The goal was to win as a team. A month after the Fullerton tournament, I and my partner, Mary Jo, were in the finals of the Ojai Valley tournament, a famous one in California. In that small box I carted around through the years was another photo. It brought memories of that final match in Ojai in April of 1958.

IV. The Gold Cup

Today I located the one tennis trophy I kept of the many I won. After graduating from USC, I headed North to San Francisco for graduate school. That year my parents decided to sell the house in Fullerton and invest the money in a small ranch in Pauma Valley near San Diego. Mother asked what I wanted done with my trophies. I said to donate them to the Fullerton Youth Tennis Foundation, which had done so much for me through the years. I knew the trophies could be reused and new plates put on them. Yet there was one tiny trophy I wanted my mother to save for me: a small gold cup, six inches high. (I just measured it with a ruler!) This cup says, "Ojai Valley Tennis Tournament, Younger Boys and Girls Championships, Girl's Doubles Runner Up, 1958."

Unlike the cup, which brings a smile to my face, the newspaper clipping from that day brings disquiet. Mary Jo and I did not expect to be in the finals. We, along with the boy's team, were allowed to miss school that week, and Terry's father had driven us to Ojai. Mary Jo and I had only a few tennis dresses.

This meant on Saturday, the day of the finals, we had to wear a dress worn before. Housed with a couple in Ojai, we had not wanted to ask about doing laundry.

On Saturday for the final, there we were in our limp dresses (cotton required an iron then). A photo was taken with our opponents, Linda Lou and Cathy Lee Crosby. My mother often reminded me to sit up straight, but it was not what I did naturally. In the photo, the Crosby sisters in their private school white blazers look as if they have rods in their backs. I mention this because private schools sent teams to the Ojai tournament, along with some public schools like Fullerton. The tournament was invitational, and youth events for those over 15 were open

Left to right: *Cathy Lee, Linda Lou, Gail, Mary Jo before the final match, Ojai, California, spring 1958.*

only to private schools. This meant Mary Jo and I had one chance to bring a blue and gold banner back to Fullerton Union High School, to be placed on the school's wall of trophies & banners for sports victories.

More bothered me the day of the finals than the prim posture of our opponents and their spotless attire. Their schoolmates, the entire private Pasadena school for girls it would seem, were nearby in the stands to watch the final. No one was there for us except the Fullerton High boy's team, Sheldon Boege and Terry Andrews, who had lost much earlier in the tournament. But Mr. Leonard, the sports-reporter for the Fullerton newspaper, was there with his notepad and camera.

My hamartia, as the Greeks would say, was and is, witnessing or experiencing injustice. I heard in kindergarten to "row your boat, gently down the stream." Later I adopted the advice of Dylan Thomas, whose hamartia was drink: "Do not go gently into the night. Rage, rage against the dying light." In the Ojai finals, Mary Jo and I were leading 5-4, 40-30, when an injustice occurred. Ojai Valley made a big deal out of this annual tournament. For our final match there were two ball boys and a referee in a fancy large hat. She had the look of a society lady, not a tennis player. Linda Lou was serving. One point and the first set would be ours. Linda served into the ad court, which I played because of my strong backhand. The serve tipped the net. I knocked it away to the ball boy. The referee called, "Deuce." I could not believe my ears. "That was a let." I looked at Cathy at the net and assumed she would confirm this. She said nothing. The referee repeated, "Deuce." What to do? No coach to argue for us. No parents there. My father would have protested loudly. Before me was only that silent grandstand of girls in their white blazers. I unraveled. Unfairness does that to me. We lost that game and the next two, to lose the first set, 7-5. I had to resort to the article about the match to see what happened in the second set. I had assumed we lost the second set badly because my oar kept slapping the water. We lost the second set 7-5. But Mr. Leonard's article about the match in the Fullerton paper brought more bitterness. He said the team of Wilson and Conger had been outplayed at the net. This was true. But he made no mention of what had happened on the ad point for the first set. Later in college I would return to Ojai when the invitational included college players. Linda Lou and later Cathy Lee played

Left to right: *Mary Jo, Gail, Cathy Lee, Linda Lou, after the final match, Ojai, California, spring 1958.*

for USC, too. And Linda became a friend from our freshman year, when a tennis team was instigated, and she and I traveled to tournaments together.

Back in 1958, for the semi-final match on Friday, the Rumanian pro, Tanny, was there because he coached the team from Westlake, a private girls' school in Los Angeles. Mary Jo and I won in three sets, and Tanny later admitted he had felt conflicted but secretly hoped that I and my partner would win. Which we did.

Another memory of 1958 in Ojai was the night we (the four Fullerton players) went to the local movie theater and saw, *Wild is the Wind*. I had never seen a film before. I had seen movies but nothing like this. Today when I listen to Nina Simone sing the film's theme song, the experience in Ojai returns to me. Naturally, the four of us did not discuss *Wild is the Wind*. We had no language for the sexuality, the infidelity, the raw and unforgettable desire in a woman brought to Nevada from Italy to be a second wife of the widowed Anthony Quinn, and the affair that occurs with his son. The stuff of Greek tragedy, but four freshmen in high school had no notion of that either.

I sit here on Friday morning, January 28th in 2023, humming the film's song, knowing a computer guru will arrive later to assemble a new Dell. Thus, I am in a rush to finish one more "uneasy" piece and get it sent off to the brilliant & artistic Cort Sinnes in the Napa Valley. Cort was my student in Napa, eleven years after this match in Ojai. Soon I will face Word Eleven. I live in 'future shock'; and the currents of this technological sea are drowning me. I only forget the slosh of waves when I run freely on a tennis court, or lift a pen, or place fingers on a keyboard, as I have now, and give form to thoughts, to see where memory and movement might lead me. Memory as framing consciousness. Memory matters and gives back the enduring self, both changed and unchanged.

V. Men in My Life

To understand what I will relate in this fifth uneasy piece requires a swivel into the 1950s, that decade often cited with nostalgia as a time of innocence and security. Segregation is the word I think of, racial and social.

My mother, for example, had no male friends. Couples, yes. And before she began working when I was in junior high, Mother's time was spent with women. She was on the altar and wedding committee at the First Presbyterian church in Fullerton, did craft projects with her old friend, Sally Boege, and was a member of a bridge group comprised of friends from Long Beach. The "gals" went back to their junior high days, and when I saw them, they were to be addressed formally, "Hello Mrs. Clark." Never once did I return home from school, the tennis courts, or anywhere else and find a man seated in our living room. No male pals, in other words. Mother's eventual employment in the medical profession as a hospital admitting clerk and later as a physician's insurance clerk, meant deference to male physicians. To say "doctor" then was followed by the pronoun, he. I know I state the obvious to anyone my age. Back then in a small town like Fullerton, with its delineated social order, divorce was uncommon, too.

Yet tennis introduced me to a world of boys and men. I learned to be around males and think myself their equal. I had not liked my first tennis teacher, but he was the exception. I have fond memories of Herb, a school principal, who would hit tennis balls to me after his long day of work. This was during junior high and my early years of high school, when my father had serious medical problems and had stopped playing tennis. On weekends I played tennis with local men who included me in their doubles. Eventually, I worked at Boege and Bean

INSTRUCTION FROM THE MASTER — Fred Fuller, veteran Fullerton tennis player, shows Glenda Gray, 16-year-old Fullerton High net star, and Gail Wilson, left, a few successful pointers about the game of tennis. The sports-loving businessman never took a lesson, but has given many an opponent lessons and helpful tips. Wilson and Gray are both highly-rated prospects by all tennis observers.

(Photo by Neuhauer)

Sporting Goods with the two owners and two male employees. They teased me ruthlessly, and I learned to give "it" back. A kind, elderly man, Fred Fuller, would hit balls to me or return my serves for hours. He was 70, which seemed ancient at the time. I laugh, keying these words at almost 80. And Tanny, the Rumanian pro, had me pick up balls for him while he taught and would give me extra help without charging. During junior high and early high school, I was able to stay with my aunt and uncle, whose house was not far from the courts where Tanny taught. Later, there was Oran, a junior college physical education teacher. He handled summer recreation programs and hired me

CITY CHAMPIONS — Oran Breeland awards trophies to six winners of the second annual City Boys and Girls Tennis Tournament. Left to right are Ann Crutcher, girls' B class; Jean North, girls' C; Bill Rice, boys' A; Gail Wilson, girls' A; Jim Buchiester, boys' C, and Steve Hall, boys' B class.
(Courtesy Gerald Boege)

during college. The list could go on and on. And at tournaments I had all kinds of male tennis pals.

After USC, living in San Francisco, the czar of Northern California tennis (the equivalent of czar Perry T. Jones in So Cal) helped me out. He would sit in his special chair at Golden Gate Park, watch me hit, admire my game. He hired me to teach for the Northern California Youth Tennis Foundation. In parks throughout the city during the summer of 1966, I taught lessons. I also met Cary in San Francisco. Throughout my life, if I went and hit on a backboard, someone would come and ask me to play. This happened at courts in the Marina one day. The story is worth telling because of the times. Cary hailed from Harlem and had learned to play with cracked tennis racquets on cement walls, not unlike Althea Gibson. He was a jazz musician and somehow through Robert Kennedy was given a cushy job in San Francisco, which gave him lots of time for his passion, which was tennis. He lived across the Golden Gate in Marin County, was married, and had a young son I met once to help him select a birthday gift for his mother. Cary provided new balls for us to practice with. He did not have a polished game but was a terrific athlete, fast on his feet, and with excellent reactions. When I returned after a day of teaching tennis that summer of 1966, Cary would show up at Golden Gate Park to hit with me, then give me a ride to Twin Peaks where I was living at the time.

One late afternoon we played during 'Singles Night' when the unmarried went to Golden Gate Park in hopes of finding someone, male or female. Cary and I had grabbed a court. A foursome of two couples were beside us. They had fancy equipment and clothing but could not play tennis. Which meant a lot of balls from their court on ours. But each time a ball rolled onto our court, Cary or I returned it. But the first time one of ours went on their court, they ignored it. I assumed this was ignorance of tennis etiquette. The second time they ignored our ball, I realized this was racial. When their next ball came on my side of the court, I picked it up and hit it over the back fence, then said, "Oh, sorry. Was that your ball?" Cary's reaction, I remember vividly. He sauntered to the net and motioned for me to join him. In his calm deep voice, this musician said seven words to me. The highest compliment I ever received. "Gail, you would make a lousy nigger."

Cary entered me in the California Public Parks annual tournament, held that year in Oakland, and almost exclusively black players. The mayor of Oakland, Lionel Wilson, was married to a Caucasian redhead. They both played tennis. He held a party at his home and Cary was invited. He asked me to go with him because I had red hair and was named Wilson! I reached the finals, then was beaten by an Althea Gibson double from Los Angeles. She stood over six feet and played the net. Except for playing against tall men, I had not played a woman that tall with such long arms and legs. She waxed me, as we used to say of an easy win. Soon after I began student teaching in fall 1966 and had no time to play tennis. I lost contact with Cary but have not forgotten him. He gave me lessons on race in America, as well as letting me know I knew nothing about jazz. It appalled him that I liked West Montgomery. He introduced me to Miles Davis and John Coltrane.

Years later, living in West Germany, I received a clipping one day from the *Napa Register*, sent by my good friend Barry, a fellow teacher and literary friend from 1969 onward. When I left Napa in 1979, he and I stayed close through correspondence, and saw each other as often as possible until Barry's death in his nineties in 2012. The clipping Barry had sent me in Germany was about my tennis pal, Dick Philbert, a math teacher in Napa. At the time he had been working a second job in a liquor store. One night it was robbed, and he and the other employee were put in the cold storage room and shot to death. To read this news on a cold winter's day in Germany was too much emotionally. I think that day was when I realized I was a writer. The only way to process this painful news was to write a letter to the editor of the Napa newspaper. For years Dick had been my mixed doubles partner and someone I practiced with regularly. He had five children and struggled on a teacher's salary. He often visited me in Soda Canyon, as we enjoyed each other's company. He had been a musician and able to play his clarinet in military bands, before he became a teacher. It was good (and still is) that husband Mike accepted from the beginning that I had both male and female friends. This is so common today and was for my daughters growing up. But as I stated at the beginning of this narrative, this was not common when I grew up.

When I moved from Lima, Peru, to Wicomico Church in the Northern Neck of Virginia in fall 2004, I wondered if I was back in Fullerton. A lovely woman in her late eighties took the first class I taught for the community college in 2005: a literature course on two deceased O'Connors, Frank from Ireland, and Flannery from Milledgeville, Georgia. Ruby Lee Norris had been an English teacher and was a writer. She told the library staff after the first class that I was a "keeper." When the course ended, I had the pleasure of seeing Ruby Lee again. In an informal meeting she said in her Virginia accent, "Gail, dear... am I to understand you play tennis with men?" She could have been asking if I ran the local bordello. I laughed and laughed. A year in a small area and already I had a reputation! It turned out I was playing tennis with a man, a good-looking one, an ex-college-basketball player, a lefty. He and I played twice a week at the Indian Creek indoor courts. He preferred to play with me, rather than the male players in the club. Eventually this man moved to Florida where there were more tennis players of his caliber. This is the man Ruby Lee had heard about. I miss this unique woman deeply, though she preferred to be called a lady! Nothing prepared me in life to have so many friends die, as occurs here at my age.

I will end with gratitude toward the four men who play tennis with me each week: Charlie, Keith, Norm, and Bill. I will add George, the pro, with whom I love to talk about tennis. Not everyone does. For Christmas I gave husband Mike four cardio sessions with George. The player I have practiced with the longest here is Norm Faulkner, a fellow lover of literature, too. Once he and I played for two hours each Thursday morning, then cut back to ninety minutes (to the detriment of our stamina, I might add). Who else would meet me at 7:00 a.m. to play tennis? Before my knees were replaced, Norm was having to be kind. Now he is less so but able to run down anything I hit, given his soccer legs and quick reactions. My only goal these days is to make him work to beat me. Keith and I smash low flat balls for ninety minutes on Wednesdays. He and Norm are youngsters, in their sixties. Charlie and Bill are in their seventies, and I feel gratitude that both play tennis with me.

In the end the man I thank is my father. Around the age of fifteen, he gave me for Christmas a figurine of a red devil, holding a gold tennis racket. I wish I still had it. I suffered from the demon of distraction. A mind with so many thoughts. How to focus only on a tennis ball? And who was I playing for? From eleven until fourteen nothing felt complicated. I wanted to win for my father. In fifth grade my mother was expecting twins. I was over the moon, even though our rented house was small and my father's salary not large. But mother did not have twins, she had two ovaries the size of grapefruit. She almost bled to death and a Catholic hospital would not allow the surgery until her Protestant physician convinced the sister-in- charge, that no babies were inside the dying patient. Mother ended up with an initial surgery to save her life and a hysterectomy months later. She was 39. And no one, at least in my family, talked openly about this. At the same time, my father had not been given the position he had sought in Sunkist. That was a blow. Father did not know a better position awaited him, which involved the export of Sunkist fruit to Europe and later to Japan. Stressful work that involved travel. Then his appendix ruptured. He entered the hospital at 170 pounds and left at 125. Medical mishaps had occurred. Then again in 1960, he almost died. I believe that Father outraged his nature; that he was meant to be a farmer, a grower, and not meant to deal with the longshoreman's union, or with Chinese in Hong Kong, and the Japanese in Tokyo. But Robert Theron Wilson admired Norwegians and in 1973, at the time of his retirement from Sunkist, a Norwegian shipping company gave him an around-the-world passage on their ships. For my mother, it was the journey of her lifetime.

I have written this book to give my father a story, to say all that I had not said while he was alive. He died at 79, the age I am now. I lament how foolish and stupid and self-possessed so many of us are, to not make time to listen deeply to those who gave us life. As Shakespeare in *King Lear* told us, "Ripeness is all." And we live a life to realize the truth of this. Then we, too, die. Yet if the soul is immortal, as Plato argued in the *Phaedo*, and the New Testament claims, and other religions believe, then my father has receptive atoms for my thanks, as does my mother.

Father would have appreciated his granddaughters, Michelle and Bonnie, if he had known them as adults. One a general, one a gardener and free spirt, both gutsy and smart. He would have liked that. And when Michelle said the following words from Samuel Beckett at her farewell from brigade command in Germany, I heard words my father would have loved.

Ever tried. Ever failed. No matter. Try again. Fail again. Fail better.

A mantra for every man and woman.

Set Three

Sisyphus on Crosshills

On the Virginia roadway I've adopted in memory of my father, I'm keenly aware of how ambivalent Father would be about his daughter picking up trash. The word resonated with him, related to a place and a time he did not easily call his own. Too many years of Dust Bowl refugees flooding California, cinematic images of *The Grapes of Wrath*, and words like Okies. I don't recall a time during my California youth when Father talked about being from Arkansas.

Odd memories come to me as I collect litter in the Northern Neck of Virginia on Route 679, known as Crosshills. One afternoon with a bulging thirty-gallon trash bag in my hand, I remembered the night when a date in an elegant San Francisco restaurant began eating a Caesar salad with his fingers, leaf by dripping leaf. Seeing my expression of disbelief, the wealthy young man said, "If you know who you are, you can eat however you like."

Such privileged insouciance was not my father's birthright. He never shed an old coat of the rural, segregated South, and the unease of being thought, *white trash*. As a young man living

131

in southern California in the late 1920s, Robert Wilson went to college on a basketball scholarship at a university for rich kids. In a photo at the University of Southern California, my father is surrounded by handsome young men from the SAE fraternity house, all elegantly dressed in West Egg finery, sweaters tossed over their shoulders. My father's sweater looks ill-shaped and has a hole in one sleeve.

One day as I collected trash on Crosshills, a former student came to mind from a class I student-taught outside San Francisco in1966. A year later, Sue surprised me in southern California, arriving in Haight-Ashbury attire, with a stash of pot in her backpack. What was the probability of running into my father in a tiny Mexican restaurant in Palos Verdes? Mother was away at the time, and Father had gone out to eat. Sue and I were already in a booth when I saw him sit down at the counter. I assumed at some point he would swivel on the stool and see me. So I walked over and invited him to join us. My memory of that meal is like a dry, bean burrito stuck in my throat. Later Father said that he hadn't paid for college so I could rescue "street people."

Recently, my neighbor stopped while I was gathering litter on Crosshills. "They'll throw trash just to spite you," he said, without identifying *they*. Shortly after he said this, someone sprayed angry epithets on several adopt-a-highway signs on Route 200. Hostility seems woven into littering. To open a car window and toss the remains of a meal, right down to the tiny packets of pepper and salt: Can this be unconscious behavior? Often on my adopted roadway, people dump household garbage, old tires, and automotive parts. Once I found a rusted wheelbarrow and hauled that to the dump.

As I gather trash, there is no accounting for the images that come to mind. *Alice's Restaurant?* Didn't Arlo Guthrie's film character get arrested because his litter was found in a dumpster where it didn't belong? This memory led to a fantasy of finding evidence that identified a litterbug, although what my action would be wasn't clear until I came across envelopes from the Department of Labor, addressed to a man whose post office box was a row away from mine. So I wrote Clarence a note, returned his several envelopes, said I hoped he hadn't meant to leave his mail on Crosshills.

> One aging woman.
> One long stretch of roadway in a county
> and country strewn with trash.
> Sisyphean.

This word came to me one day when my neighbor stopped a second time and called out: "You'll be doing that forever." It was his comment that made me think of Sisyphus, whose punishment in Hades was to roll a boulder uphill eternally. Sisyphean: endless, heart-breaking work. Accounts vary as to Sisyphus's misdeeds, but one unrelated fact is clear: My behaviour with my father was often adolescent, not unlike the actions of those who throw trash to spite those picking it up.

Like my father, I've lead a migratory life, absorbing traditions of other cultures. Yet by the time I moved to Malaysia in the late 80s, Father was dead, and I regretted that I'd not asked him more about his work in Asia. Even though I was in California to attend my father's memorial service, I wasn't there when Mother spread his ashes among their avocado trees. Yet from living in Asia among the Chinese, I'd observed the practice of ancestral shrines, of creating a place to honor ancestors. For Robert Theron Wilson, an ancestral shrine had to be outdoors, as nature was his religion. A storm could wipe out his avocado crop, but he accepted the devastation with a stoical attitude I admire.

Now.

For many seniors, memory is a litter that exhibits a worrisome tendency to live in the past. Yet my father relished old stories of his foreign travel, which began during college when he took a year off and worked on a tramp steamer for free passage to Europe. In a small journal, he recorded his adventure of traveling around the continent in the early 30s. Decades later, when Sunkist Growers began exporting fruit to Europe and later to Asia, my father spent long periods abroad. He even devised the system for pallets that kept exported citrus from spoilage.

One day last winter, as I traversed a barren Crosshills, I thought of a last walk with my father. He and my mother had driven to Vacaville, California, following Father's open heart surgery. As he and I walked in an area of new homes, I noticed how he was shuffling—the only way I knew how weak he was from the operation. Although he rallied, Father soon began to decline. His surgery was before the widespread news about AIDS. I picture a desperate soul, a drug user or prostitute, selling his or her blood in San Diego. No testing of blood in 1983 for HIV. Two years later, was it AIDS that took my father's life? My mother's request for an autopsy was not granted: she had wanted to know why her husband recovered from surgery, then fell into a lethargy so deep he couldn't get up to work on the ranch. There were strange lesions on his body, too. Eventually hospitalized with an infected lining of the heart, Father wasn't treated with antibiotics, as if his death were a foregone conclusion. He died alone in a hospital in Escondido, with my mother having left for the night. My brother was not there either; and I was away in Germany with my family. As I walk my stretch of scenic Virginia Byway, that bears my father's name on four signs, I think about his final moments and what it means to die alone.

Recently, I heard an interview with the British author Julian Barnes and took note of something he said. Until his late thirties he had seldom thought about death. But after he turned forty, he couldn't believe he had ever thought of anything else. Unlike this writer, I began thinking about death very early in life, which is why I found comfort in the eternal motion of waves as I wandered the shore in early morning at Newport Beach where my family spent two weeks each June. Enchanted by foam and spume, and sand bars on which I walked into the Pacific, I also began noticing flotsam and jetsam, and the seagulls diving into it. Today, when I see advertisements for cruise ships, I think about their waste polluting the oceans. In my childhood, ships dumped garbage at sea, which high tide distributed and low tide revealed: orange peels, celery stalks, tin cans, and a residue of tar that stuck to bare feet.

Have I been noticing trash my entire life?

"Hey, bag lady," my neighbor Kay called out one day. For ten years this woman's church adopted Crosshills. She spoke of the experience unfavorably. It was hard to recruit help, she said.

But more than that, they would throw trash even as she and other volunteers picked it up. Recalling her words, I recognize how easy it would be to debase those who heave trash and garbage on roadways. Yet in the Northern Neck, I'm finding claimants of "they'll throw trash just to spite you" similar to persons in the U.S. Embassy in Caracas, who expressed dismay that I worked with incarcerated Americans, all of whom were imprisoned on drug-related offenses. Mules, scum bags: I heard those words often. The stereotypes of drug users seldom held any truth, and the memory serves to remind me not to judge those who litter, even though I can count on two hands the number of water bottles I've found while beer bottles number in the hundreds. Thus far on Crosshills, I haven't come across any dead animals. The other day I read an interview with the writer Barry Lopez, who described removing dead animals from roadways as a gesture of kindness, so cars will not hit the creatures that feed on carrion. Through this action, Lopez believes a person honors both the animal and nature.

In his years after retirement, when my father had a small ranch in California's Pauma Valley, he religiously fed quail, waiting each evening at dusk for a covey to come in. Only now have I begun to understand why Father patiently sat and watched quail. In so many ways he and I are alike: our impatience with pretense, our need to tell stories whether anyone wants to hear them or not; and at the end of a thin stretch of time, a father and a daughter happy to feed birds, relish sunsets, and wade in tides of memory.

"I have had to learn the simplest things last, which made for difficulties," the poet Charles Olson wrote.

Driving past corn and soybean fields in the Northern Neck of Virginia, I like to sing "My Way" with the soulful, foot-stomping, Spanish-singing Gipsy Kings. *Regrets, I've had a few.* One is that my father read only one of my books, a short work used in literacy programs in which I fictionalized my great-great grandfather's 1849 Gold Rush letters. Father pointed out that I had mistaken Cape Hope for Cape Horn. That was it. He wasn't a man to heap praise on me, which means I feel no need for drivers to stop and thank me for removing the trash from Crosshills. I do this because it's Sisyphean: climbing in order to descend, then climbing again, struggling to be just a bit kinder and wiser.

All is still this Sunday morning, as I listen to Gregorian Chants and look at the marshlands of Mill Creek. The last piece I wrote for money was on a Peruvian potter. The artist loved it, as did I, until the editor left her irksome changes on every page. "Forget the commercial world," a writer-friend recently told me. "Write to make discoveries."

Hearing her words, I asked myself: *What are the fragments for if not to be rejoined?* So here I sit, an archeologist of the spirit, digging into the past, fingers in a remembered desert, trying to reshape an urn, studying rediscovered pieces to see how they fit together. How very different from finding tiny liquor bottles in brown paper sacks, or the remains of fast food, right down to the salt and catsup: Modern trash, not ancient earthen vessels. Yet to discover who you are, what formed you, what shape fragments have given to life: This is what I seek as I traverse the miles on Crosshills, between signs that say, *In Memory of Robert T. Wilson.*

The Orthopedic, a Literary Loving Patient, and Julian Barnes

Dear Dr. Nordt,   July 21, 2020
I first visited your office over a decade ago. Pointing to an X-ray, you said, "Your knee is shot, kiddo." Then you suggested I try injections in both knees, and something called an "unloader" brace on my left knee. I saw you only one other time, when your P.A. John was unavailable to give me the third shot in my twice-yearly series of three injections. During that second visit, you read about me on the computer screen and asked if I was still playing tennis. I told you I was. "Doubles?" you asked. "No, mostly singles." You walked to the doorway and turned to face me. "You're an idiot. Better stay thin."

When I first visited John, he told me the longest someone had kept having injections was ten years. I like challenges, so I decided to match the record. Then around the fifth or sixth year, I received a call from your Ortho Virginia office. John was leaving your practice and moving to South Carolina. Another patient received the same call, and this resident of the Northern Neck told me an orthopedic in Tappahannock had a terrific P.A. like John, and the drive was shorter than Richmond. Then in 2019 this orthopedic said I'd reached the "end of my rope," and he wanted to replace both knees in the same week. Then by chance at the Shoe Clinic in Kilmarnock one day, I met the aunt of the store's manager. I'd bought countless orthopedic-designed shoes for tennis there. The manager suggested that I ask her aunt about double-knee surgery. This woman was younger than I, and she regretted her decision, adding there was no way she could run, only walk. Soon after that day, a physical therapist I respected, told me that double-surgery was a terrible idea for me. My internist, Dr. Monge-Meberg, looked pleased when I said I'd decided to return to your practice for knee replacement.

Finally, this leads me to the British writer, Julian Barnes. I saw you in September 2019 and indicated I would like my left knee replaced as soon as possible, though it could not be in October. Earlier you had looked at the computer screen and said, "Long time since we've seen you." Then you asked me why October was out. I said I would be teaching a course that month on the British writer, Julian Barnes. You said nothing. But from the doorway you asked if this British writer was dead or alive? I told you he was alive and well in London.

It is not unusual for me to send books, even to people I do not know well or at all. And something told me to send you, *The Noise of Time*, one of the novels I was using in my course. It's a perfect book for our times, given we had a bloviated President who was fond of Putin and the Russians. The book is, as you now know, a fact-fiction novel about Shostakovich and Stalin's brutal tyrannical times. When you sent me $16.00 in cash for the book, I was bemused. Which is why on the day of the surgery, my husband gave you *Levels of Life* by Barnes.

At present you have a collection of four works by Sir Julian. They include the first two I just mentioned, along with *Sense of an Ending*, plus *Arthur and George*. Now I am giving you his

139

latest book about a famous physician in France during the *Belle Epoque*. It is a factual work for the most part, best read a few pages at a time. Also, one of my students gave me this new copy of *The Lemon Table*, which I used in the October class on Barnes. I think you will enjoy these fictional stories. A few are wildly funny. Not all. "The Silence" is about the composer, Sibelius, though Barnes does not identify him. Another humorous one is "Knowing French," about a woman who reads *Flaubert's Parrot* by Barnes and begins to correspond through letters with him. Please don't think me daft for doing this with you!

The timing is curious about *The Lemon Table*. JB's good friends (Ian McEwan, Martin Amis, the late Christopher Hitchens) could not understand why their literary pal was focused on old age and death. This short story collection came out about the same time as JB's treatise on death, *Nothing to Be Frightened Of.* Both books appeared before Julian's wife & literary agent learned she had a brain tumor. Within a month, she died. Perhaps Julian's way to come to terms with his wife's death was to write, *Levels of Life*, the finest book I have read on grief.

My gift of books, Dr. Nordt, is to thank you for giving me two straight legs and a renewed spirit. Now I will be able to run around a tennis court again, in the time that remains. My luck was to wind my way back to your practice, and for you to have a fine professional connection to Dr. Monge-Meberg.

Each Monday I post on a new website. I dislike the word, blog, but that is the word used these days. My subject is *Literature I've Loved,* a one-page, quick read. Not Julian Barnes but readable!

With gratitude, Gail Wilson Kenna

OrthoVirginia   William E. Nordt, III, M.D.

Dear Mrs Kennan —

Thank you again for expanding my
library of Julian Barnes' works. Thanks to
you, he is the most popular author on
my shelves.

I share your concerns in the upcoming
election and recommend plenty of
exercise to vent your frustration + anxieties
— 2 new knees should help!

your literature
— Bill Nordt

P.S. I looked up "bloviate" and plan
to use it with sparkling frequency.

September 23, 2020
Dear Dr. Nordt,
Yesterday a woman named Kathleen left the indoor tennis facility
as I entered it. Her husband had seen you the day before. She
told me about her husband's fractured kneecap, then added that
you had spoken about me during their appointment. I think

Kathleen assumed this must be related to my return to tennis at eight weeks after both knee replacements. I knew otherwise. "It's not about my knees," I said. "Our connection is the writer, Julian Barnes." But Kathleen, unlike you, did not turn and ask me, as you did one year ago, about this writer.

I would have sent you a new copy of *Nothing to Be Frightened Of*, but I had given my book to a tennis pal who likes Barnes! Anyway, for the course last October I bought a used copy of *Nothing*. This morning I reread what I'd underlined last September. For lines to quote, this non-fiction work is priceless. As I said in my earlier letter, Barnes wrote this book, along with *The Lemon Table*, before his wife Patricia's death.

A student and good friend, Ilona, read *Nothing* last fall before the class on Barnes. Some of the marks in a second handwriting belong to her. I found *Nothing to Be Frightened Of* an important book for *Noise of Time* because of the many anecdotes in *Noise* about Russian composers. Julian might find the conjunction of you, me, and his literature reflective of what he says about accidents on page 185 in *Nothing*. Had I not accidently run into your patient's wife yesterday, I would not be writing this note and sending this book. The story of how I returned to your practice after a five-plus-year absence is about mysterious circumstances and accidental meetings.

All best to you,
Gail Wilson Kenna

Dearest Madame Kenna —

. I had hoped to complete your most recent allotment of reading materials and include in a thank you note a critical review profused with wit — however, after weeks of witless quiet I can wait no longer and with bone-deep gratitude, hereby thank you in advance of a proper note

(Dr) Bill Nordt

Dear Dr. Nordt,   June, 2021

Once again, I say thanks for giving me new knees. Now I can run for wide shots on a tennis court, successfully get to short shots, and make good returns. Each week I play singles with four different men (all younger). I recently had my 78th birthday but don't feel this age on a tennis court. Serendipity returned me to your practice in September 2019 for a consult, and mysterious circumstances had led me back to Parham Road. One day I might tell the story of Julian Barnes, Dr. Nordt, and a patient who brazenly sent her orthopedic surgeon a copy of *Noise of Time.* Why? Because you paused in the doorway to ask about

Julian Barnes, thus displaying a curiosity I could not ignore. Yet if I am being truthful, I will admit that I wanted you to know whose left knee you were replacing that December morning in 2019. And how can I take leave of your practice without adding one more book to your Julian collection? This is another of his short stories. I agree with the reviewer who wrote, "The stories in *Pulse* sneak up on a reader and you cannot help but be moved."

Would Julian Barnes be pleased that I am giving you Edmund De Waal's *The Hare with Amber Eyes?* I think he would. Julian writes about art and would know De Waal. And Edmund's family memoir begins in Paris in the late 1800s, a period Barnes has written about often. By the way, this is a used copy of *Hare.* The other De Waal book, *Letters to Camondo*, was recently published and should be read after *Hare.* As a gift of thanks, one book needed to be new and unmarked, but I admit to having read *Camondo* before I gift-wrapped it.

Cheers to you, Gail Kenna

• • •

On three thin sheets of paper, the following written in pencil had no date. My friend Dorie had seen Dr. Nordt to schedule a knee replacement. When he realized she knew me, he went to his office and returned with the following numbered thoughts.

1. This thank-you note comes with much gratitude for the bouquet of fine reading material you have gifted me. I apologize for not writing sooner. I had hoped to finish all my assignments but have yet to complete the short stories.

2. On the occasions that I find myself in literary company, I love to boost that I've read many of his (Julian Barnes) books. I'll throw a quote into the conversation, like, "Love is the meeting point of truth and magic," just to sound smart.

3. BTW, one of my favorite authors is Ian McEwan, another witty Brit. I'd be interested in your comparative analysis.

4. I'm particularly grateful for Edmund De Waal's books. What a gifted writer & artist he is. Probably the most interesting Art History book I've ever encountered. I read "Hare" in Cape May, on the porch of a Victorian house, awnings flapping, oft times napping (I'm a poet!). And *Camondo* is abstractly beautiful. I'll need your tutelage on that one. Not sure I fully understand it.

5. I confess to have never read *Moby Dick*. I once gave it a go via books-on-tape. After ½ hour my kids nearly jumped out of the mini-van and that was the end of that.

6. As to how one follows my wife (an artist), she says Nordt family farm on Instagram. Also, we have our annual spring party in April. If you will kindly remember to remind me to remember to invite you, I would deeply appreciate it.

7. Don't over-do it on the knees.

Sincerely, Bill Nordt

Update! Finished *Why Read Moby Dick*. Outstanding. I found myself reading long excerpts to my wife. Thanks for that!

• • •

Dear Reading Pal and Favorite Orthopedic,
I have in front of me your letter, which my good friend Dorie gave me on Sunday. Everything you wrote interested me until I reached number seven. I would require more explanation as to what constitutes over-doing it on the knees. With new ones I run as if pushed by a strong wind. Before with bowed legs, I hobbled. I've insufficient words to express the joy I feel on a tennis court these days. I hit with four men weekly, as I might have said before. We don't play games and sets, just points and tie breakers, and all in good fun. However, these are men, and they prefer to win, and especially not to lose to a woman, especially one who is almost 79.

You made me laugh with your comment about the *Moby Dick* tape and your kids wanting to flee the minivan. But now you have read Nathaniel Philbrick's book of Melville's whaling saga. I knew intuitively that you would like *The Hare with Amber Eyes.* Here's another conjunction (Julian's often-used term). One of my favorite writers is Ian McEwan. I taught the course on Julian Barnes because prior to that one, I'd offered a class, *Four Short Novels About Men.* The novels and writers were: *A River Runs Through It* by Norman Maclean, Ian McEwan's *On Chesil Beach*, Julian's *The Sense of an Ending*, and Philip Roth's *Everyman*. After that class, many students requested a course just on Barnes. I have it in mind to offer one on Ian McEwan. I don't know if you know that Barnes, McEwan, Martin Amis, and the late Christopher Hitchens comprised a group that met regularly for lunch. Can you imagine that collective wit?

The enclosed WSJ article is related to the piece I am sending with this letter. In our PC world, it is not as if I can sell, "A Sure Way to Gain Weight." But I hope it brings a laugh or two from you. You have my permission to photocopy and distribute it in your "waiting" rooms. My friend Dorie said she had forgotten to have a book with her on Friday and kept reading info charts on the walls while waiting to see you. Charts of course, are safer than a cheeky essay on the increasingly corpulent United States of America.

Cheers and thanks, Gail Kenna

A Sure Way to Gain Weight

One day in a rural Virginia post office, the woman at the head of the line had multiple problems with her mail, which made the wait a long one. I began flipping through an old *New Yorker* that someone had left on the counter. In it was an article, "The Fast Track," about seclusion in the Mojave Desert at a holistic spa called *We Care*, where famous L.A. celebrities spend a fortune to fast and to have colonic hydrotherapy.

Reading the article made me look more carefully at the three women in line ahead of me. One woman was huge but solid, unlike the young woman in front of her who must have weighed close to 300 pounds. The short, older woman holding up the line was dressed in thin cotton pedal pushers and a tank top. Two hundred pounds would be a kind estimate. The former postmaster, at that time years ago, was rotund. This meant eighty percent of the five women in the post office were gorbellied.

Later that day I finished the article on the fast-track spa where starlets go before the Academy Awards to obtain the lean and hungry look. Reading about them brought to my mind a memorable scene from Mike Nickol's movie *The Graduate*, when Mr. Robinson tells Benjamin to remember one word for America's corporate future: "Plastics." If corporate is changed to corporeal and elastic substituted for plastics, we have the country's current landscape. Americans are always making discoveries and, many decades ago, we hit on a sure way to gain weight.

Elasticized waistbands.

What's brilliant about elastic is how it supports illusions. A regular, fitted waistband is no friend, uncomfortably reminding the wearer that he or she is gaining weight. Why? Hefty, mid-section rolls are both seen and felt. Doesn't discomfort from a tight waistband help curb the appetite? I remember my southern California hometown's first 'all you can eat' restaurant. What an absurd notion to think you could eat all you wanted. Even at Thanksgiving the fitted clothing we wore made it unwise, if not impossible, to eat everything on a holiday-laden table.

If my reader thinks I harbor a prejudice toward those who are overweight, the assumption is wrong. I was a chunky kid, and as a teen I could have spent my life in a movie theatre, eating popcorn, and waddling around in sweatpants. The first time I saw the film adaptation of the British writer Evelyn Waugh's, *The*

Loved One, there was a moment of recognition. In one scene, Joyboy's mother, who is too bovine to leave her bed, rips into an entire turkey or roasted pig and the fat and skin start flying around the bedroom. In Waugh's depiction of America's fat mama, I saw myself. More than once, Mother had caught me ripping the crackling skin off a turkey as it cooled before it was carved. In childhood whenever I heard the song, "Blue Moon," I thought of blue cheese. Fortunately, I confronted my problem of over-eating and realized early on that elastic encourages the habit. As a competitive tennis player, even five extra pounds slowed me down on the court.

Unfortunately, the norm in America, the land of expansion, is against moderation and restraint. Is obesity our manifest destiny, which we're achieving through huge servings and super-size soft drinks? Youth in the USA who relish fast food and snacks can toddle off to school in baggy pants and oversized clothing. In Colombia and Peru, where I lived before moving to the Northern Neck of Virginia, I observed that schoolgirls wore short-pleated skirts with their blouses tucked in. There was no elastic in the waistbands of the uniforms, and the pleats were meant to be flat, not protruding. It's difficult to imagine an overweight American girl in this attire. Yet fitted clothing might be an incentive to order the kiddy meal instead of the lumberjack special.

Years ago, I saw a PBS biography on General Douglas MacArthur. Except for footage of President Taft trying to hoist his elephantine self onto a horse, I don't recall another overweight person in four hours of footage. Women's clothing sizes were few then. In the 1930s and 40s, my mother wore a size 12. By the

1960s I wore a size 10 and my mother, whose weight hadn't changed for decades, was wearing size 8. Today although I'm the same weight as before, a size 2 is often too large, and my mother before her death had difficulty finding small enough clothing to fit her. When my daughter, a size 2, studied in Spain and asked for "small," slender clerks laughed. By Spain's standards, my daughter was a medium. Recently, in San Francisco, I tried on a pair of one-hundred-dollar slacks, only to see if I could fit in size zero. Not even snug. What, I ask, is going on with the sizing of women's clothing? Paradoxical, isn't it? Women get larger and the sizes get smaller. In *Health* magazine in the column, "Best Shape/I Did It," is the story of a young woman who lost 171 pounds by changing some of her habits. Once she weighed 318 pounds and wore size 28. Now, to her credit, she weighs 147 and wears size 4. My point is not to diminish her success—only to note that sizing keeps shrinking. The old 14 is the new 4.

In my youth, few people in my southern California community were fat and few were thin. Now, especially among young women, the extremes are shocking. Years ago, I worked in a summer program at Georgetown University with high school students interested in becoming medical doctors. On one side of my dorm room were two young women of such enormity that I had to wonder how they envisioned being doctors. On the other side, a girl left each morning at five for a run, then ate one-half slice of pineapple at breakfast. Her legs were as thin as my arms. A year earlier I'd taught at American University where someone had the bright idea that students could elect a course that met in the dorm so they might wear pajamas to class. This is only to say that our ubiquitous 'relaxed' attire has not come free of charge in the USA.

In claiming that elastic is an ally of overeating, I am not ignoring the commonly recognized causes of our national problem with obesity: trans-fats, sugar and fructose, snacking, stress, inadequate exercise, and America's huge portions. And now the pandemic and being home near the refrigerator too much of the time. There is air conditioning too, which is no foe of fat. It used to be that everyone I knew dropped weight during summer. Who wanted to turn on the oven when the house was already 100 degrees? So, we ate salads and fruit. Now, thanks to AC for almost everyone, it's possible to eat all year as if it's winter, with a little prehistoric voice whispering, "Time to pad the fat cells." But given these realities, it's also safe to assume the burgeoning masses of the overweight are elasticized.

Back when I lived in the Napa Valley, I had a friend who loved cats. Her country home housed a dozen felines. Big bowls of cat food were everywhere. Gluttony (the word is still PC for cats) presented a problem for only one feline. Well-buttoned in his fur, he ate until stretched to the limit, then took off for the hills, returning only when he was sleek and could go at the bowls again. Most of us are smarter than cats, so why aren't two things obvious? First, shun elastic. And second I say get "woke," as is said today, the word grinding away at my literate ear. My point? Clothing manufacturers are not using elastic in the waistbands of men's suits, are they? And the U.S. Army has gone back to fitted jackets, circa WW2. Seems to me a clever way to control burgeoning military waistlines.

I will end, tongue in cheek, by saying this. If fasting at *We Care* in the Mojave Desert is a Hollywood dream, then except when you're exercising and wearing comfortable sports attire, think seriously about eliminating elastic from your life.

• • •

Ortho Virginia sought responses from patients to share stories about their surgical experiences. I responded to the request through their portal, and then received a phone call from a communications director. She asked me to send them a piece about Dr. Nordt for the Ortho Virginia website. The following is what I wrote.

I would like to share a story about William E. Nordt, the Third, a prince of an orthopedic, who can only be called 'royal'. Why does a woman of 79 years say this? In December 2019, my left knee was replaced. Then in June 2020, I was given a new right one. For over a decade, I fought against having my knees replaced. I wanted to break a ten-year record I'd been told about by the P.A. in Dr. Nordt's practice. Which means I kept having twice yearly injections, three weeks in a row, equivalent to a lube job on rusty automotive parts. The shots worked. But injections did not stop my legs from bowing. It seemed unlikely I would stand again with my legs touching each other.

Since age ten, I have played competitive tennis. I was a ranked player in Southern California, and a teaching pro for many years. My goal was to die in old age on a tennis court while running for a shot. But my bowed legs kept me from running except in a slow and awkward way. Desperation led me back to Dr. Nordt's practice after getting shots elsewhere for five years. I only left his practice because his P.A. moved to South Carolina. This was the same period when the royal orthopedic, William the Third, learned an advanced, computerized way to replace knees. In September 2019, Dr. Nordt looked at my old file on his computer and said, "Long time since we've seen you."

After the first surgery that early December, I was back on the tennis court after eight weeks. And following the second replacement six months later, I could again run freely. Do you have any idea what this means to a woman of 79? To run fast, to change directions, to move forward and back, to pivot and know that beneath me are two strong, straight legs? I've inadequate words for the joy I feel with revitalized movement.

Where I live, in the Northern Neck of Virginia, William E. Nordt, M.D. is well known. His name resonates as the orthopedic to see in Richmond. What luck that my stars aligned in fall 2019 when I returned to his Ortho Virginia practice. Now, each time I step on a tennis court or get out of bed in the morning, I give thanks to this unique man for his skills as an orthopedic surgeon, for his sense of humor, and his exceptional taste in fine literature.

• • •

April 2022 email exchange:

April 4th Dorie to Gail Kenna, Subject: *Elizabeth Finch* by Julian Barnes

April 9…New book by Julian Barnes. This sent from Dorie to Gail to Dr. Nordt, with cheers

April 9 reply from Dr. Nordt…Wonderful news (new novel). Nordt party on April 30th, should your awards engagements change.

Sunday, April 10…Still going to D.C. for the conference and sorry to miss the annual picnic. Last week I responded to a request on the Ortho Virginia site to share a story. I wrote a beginning and said to contact me if anyone wanted the whole piece. Margaret contacted me and sent forms to sign. I hope what I wrote makes you laugh, or I won't get an invite to the festivities at the farm next April. What I wrote is all true.

Good thoughts, Gail Kenna

• • •

Hi Ms. Kenna   April 26
1. I have achieved a pinnacle when an author writes a piece about me. For that I thank you.
2. Being the recipient of the modifier "courtly" places me among

history's rarest surgeons—an elevation you've given me that equals the swiftness in your feet.

3. Thank you for the xeroxed intros and chapters, complete with the critic's pen of underlines, parentheses, circles, asterisks and smiley faces, a sophisticated system of yours I am learning to decipher.

4. I am fortunate to have you as a patient and friend.

Bill Nordt.

June 5, 2022 to Gail Kenna

Hi Mrs. Kenna, As a brief literary update, my family and I vacationed in Maine where I read "Our Country Friends" (Gary Shteyngart) and "On Earth We're Briefly Gorgeous"(Ocean Vuong), and both have merits. Went to a bookstore in Portland and almost picked up "England, England" by your sweetheart, but by this time I'd had enough fiction and opted for "The Religious Revolution," which is an exceptional historical analysis. I await your next command.

Sincerely, Bill Nordt

June 5 to Dr. Nordt...

Dear Voracious Reader, The latest by Julian is a short novel you will receive as soon as Dorie reads it and I reread it. The novel is only available in the UK, and you will receive a signed copy. It will be a curious one for you to read, and a bit ironic given you recently bought *The Religious Revolution.* In this fact-fiction novel, Barnes has created a memorable teacher, Elizabeth Finch, and given readers a history lesson on Julian the Apostate. Only Barnes could pull this off.

•   •   •

My last blog was on physician-writers; and tomorrow I will write again on Dr. Anton Chekhov, one of my literary heroes. That's all from the Northern Neck and from your patient who turned 79 today. I hope it was a fine vacation in Maine. All best to you and your family.

Gail Kenna

Dear Prince William,   August 12, 2022

Kilmarnock's Lancaster Library often has used book sales. A patron is allowed to fill a grocery bag (I use one from Trader Joe's) for $5.00. You do the math on what these two books that sold originally for $35.00, cost me! Note: In my bag I had your two and ten others.

The one on words has a hopeful inscription from a grandmother to her granddaughter. I covered it up. Could be removed with a razor! The book with a poem a day is one I gave to Dr. Monge-Meberg a few years ago. I was delighted to find another copy at the book sale. Patricia and daughter Rebecca had "bonding" time doing a daily poem, she told me. Just this week, Rebecca left for college to study marine biology in Florida. For graduation I gave her a fine copy of *Moby Dick* to save her from

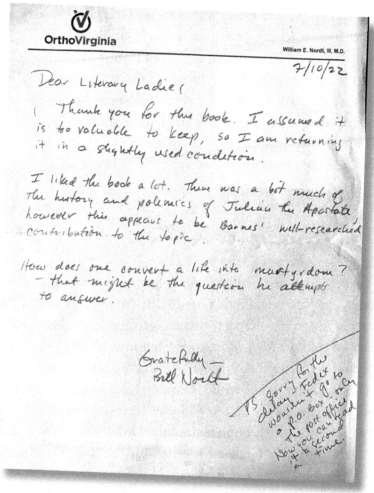

OrthoVirginia

William E. Nordt, III, M.D.

7/10/22

Dear Literary Ladies

Thank you for this book. I assumed it is too valuable to keep, so I am returning it in a slightly used condition.

I liked the book a lot. There was a bit much of the history and polemics of Julian the Apostate, however this appears to be Barnes' well-researched contribution to the topic.

How does one convert a life into martyrdom? — that might be the question he attempts to answer.

Gratefully —
Bill Nordt

PS Sorry for the delay — Fedex wouldn't go to a P.O. box, only the post office. Now you can read it a second time.

having to buy a textbook on whales.

The famous German Goethe admonished everyman and woman to read a poem a day and listen to some fine music. I think you and I would agree. So would Ilona Duncan, the patient who will give you this bag. She is my good friend, a student in

157

my classes, the webmaster who posts my blog each Monday, and once wrote a letter to our literary pal, Julian Barnes.

I trust all is well with you and your family in these increasingly strange times. Elizabeth Finch would say, "When weren't they worrisome and crazy?" For sanity I run often on a tennis court and feel gratitude for obliging knees and mysterious conjunctions, as Julian Barnes would say.

My best thoughts with you, always,

Gail Kenna

Saturday, November 12, e-mail to Dr. Nordt

A quick question. I am compiling for family, friends, and avid tennis players, a collection related to tennis, and would like permission to include some of our correspondence. I just pulled out Julian's *The Only Story*, to remind myself to tell Cort, my book designer in the Napa Valley, to take a look at the novel's cover with its wood tennis racquet. Yet another connection between you, Julian Barnes, and your literary-loving Gail/Gale. I will include the short piece from the Ortho Virginia website.

I so love fall. Hope all is well with you and your family. With ever-present gratitude, Gail

P.S. I've started a RCC-RILL book club for 2023. Attaching a photo of the books. Five sessions and two novels each time this coming year.

•   •   •

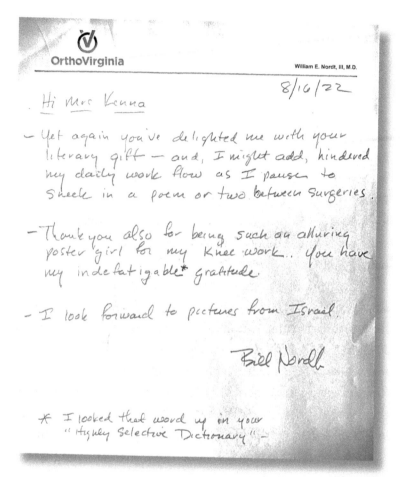

OrthoVirginia   William E. Nordt, III, M.D.

8/16/22

Hi Mrs Kenna

— Yet again you've delighted me with your literary gift — and, I might add, hindered my daily work flow as I pause to sneek in a poem or two between surgeries.

— Thank you also for being such an alluring poster girl for my knee work.. You have my indefatigable* gratitude.

— I look forward to pictures from Israel.

Bill Nordt

* I looked that word up in your "Highly Selective Dictionary" —

Hi Ms. Kenna,   11/13/22

You have my permission, though I wouldn't think you need it. Your words are your words. Sounds like a fun project.

I believe your success has been your "inner bounce." Those who have it, out-perform their peers.

When I retire, many years from now, I plan to attend your book club, so hold a place.

• • •

Dear Dr. Nordt,

My friend is scheduled to see you on Wednesday. And today with snow falling, I am writing you this note and will get it to Dorie. Just over two years ago, you provided me with a new left knee, and six months later, a new right. And thanks to you and your laudatory skill as an orthopedic, I run as if enacting my name, Gail/Gale.

Who should I come across the other day in the London Review of Books? None other than, Sir Julian. Therefore (being formal) I am giving you another literary gift for your library. A good copy of *Madame Bovary*. Rest assured I have a pen-marked copy of Flaubert's famous novel. Another habit of mine (besides giving away books) it to clip articles and put them in the relevant book in my library. Which is why you will find in *Madame Bovary*, two articles. I reread them earlier, while in a Sunlighten sauna, which I value more than anything in this house except my husband.

Earlier at 140 infrared degrees, I realized one part of one article is missing. I discovered this when I reached the part about *Flaubert's Parrot*. I don't think I passed on this novel by Barnes to you. The other article on Flaubert is a helpful one to read. Somewhere in my library, scattered throughout the house, is a copy of *Sentimental Education* by Flaubert. The article states that Ford Maddox Ford read this novel fourteen times, which suggests I need to read *Sentimental Education* again.

I hope you and your family are all well.

Good cheer, Gail Kenna

Hi Mrs Kenna

— Just a small pay-back for the vast pages of enjoyment you have given me. (... and if you loath Franzen or already own it, please re-gift promptly to the needy). I

Meanwhile, thank you for the most recent reading allotment; your Keats collection is impressive. You are a confident professional (like me) and a fine foe of fat, indeed.

— Bill Nordt

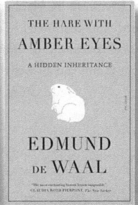

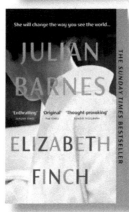

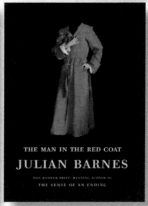

On these pages: *The contribution of fifteen fine books to William A. Nordt's library, with an emphasis on the works of Julian Barnes.*

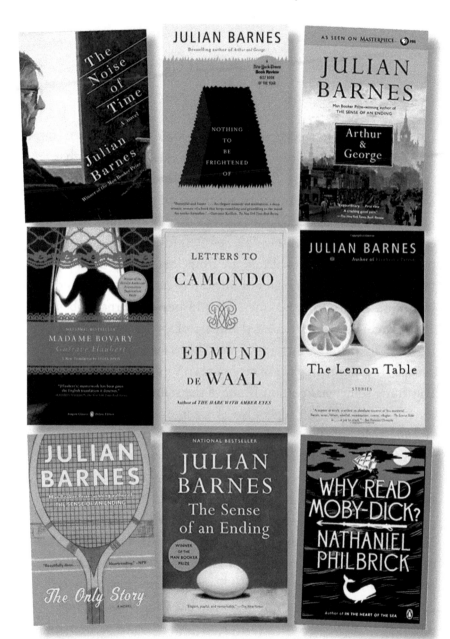

A Tennis Player & Spy, and His Ukranian Plate

C onnection, recollection, memory waiting in things. I know little of the plate's history—only that George's family fled their homeland at the end of WW 2 as greater Russian forces advanced on already occupied Kiev. His family headed West, George's mother wearing a large coat into which she had sewn her jewelry. Inside their car were small objects of traditional folk art from their native Ukraine, including two identical plates of intricately carved wood, inlaid with mother-of-pearl, and tiny stones in brown, burnt umber, and turquoise—a multi-colored mosaic of circles and squares, mystical in pattern. Sixty-two years later, one of the plates occupied a prominent place in my home on Virginia's Chesapeake Bay, hung somewhat perilously above the staircase to the lower level, a fitting location suggestive of George's clandestine work and the early exile from his homeland.

As I write these words, I'm looking at a pocket-sized photo of George. Who could resist his haunting blue eyes, the trimmed beard with its hint of gray, the burning cigarette, the glass of good scotch, the candy red Jag, his tales told with seductive wit? Which of the stories were real, and which were from the script of a case officer is not something I know. But in examining the photograph, holding it closer, a haunting line from poet ee cummings comes to mind: "how do you like your blue-eyed boy, mister death?"

I first met George in Kuala Lumpur (KL), the capital of Malaysia, at a U.S. Embassy tennis tournament in September 1987, a week after my family moved there. No one knew I had been a teaching pro in California tennis clubs. The embassy tourney was 'for fun', partners drawn randomly, a time limit of 15 minutes, and victory from total points scored. My partner was not a tennis player and wisely gave me the whole court. In the finals we faced crafty George with his wicked slice. He and his partner didn't win. From that day through the next few years, George and I played on the same side of the net in Malaysian tournaments.

Tennis is my final KL image of George, three years later in June 1990.

Early in his intelligence career, George lived in Paris, met a beautiful Tunisian woman named Jalila, and they married. Fluent in French, George wasn't enamored of *frogs* but liked to make bets with them. In KL he challenged a French intelligence officer that he, George, could play with a woman and beat two male *frogs*. The Frenchman bet their embassy's most expensive champagne that it was not possible. George and I won easily. The officer challenged George to a re-match, doubling the bet. This time the Frenchman showed up with a new partner, a young one who stood over 6 feet. I was 5'3, George a modest 5'9. The French had set the time at eleven on Royal Selangor's hard courts, not on the grass. The duo showed up late, another ploy to defeat us. No sane persons played tennis on a cement court at noon under the Malaysian sun. People came from all over the club to watch the duel between George and the *frogs*. I, the princess in the tale, needed to save George from himself. He and his family were leaving post in two days. George and Jalila, loved in KL and coveted by so many embassies, were being given farewell parties, which meant late nights, copious liquor, rich food. Jalila was furious with George for accepting the re-match, and she had reminded me that George's father died of a heart attack at fifty.

I have played a great deal of competitive tennis but never with more determination than that day. If the match went to three sets under the ruthless sun, I knew George would not quit. And if something happened to George, Jalila would not forgive me. Never had I met a woman so in love with a man in body, heart, and soul.

What was the last thing I heard from George the day of our re-match, which we won in two sets? "Get those damn bottles from the *frog*." The French intelligence officer had failed to bring the champagne with him. That's how confident he had been of victory.

Early in 1992, George visited us in Caracas at our new embassy posting. He, Jalila, and their daughters were living in Miami, where George had been sent to quietly retire after he lost a posting to Bangkok. The KL station chief claimed George lacked any new tricks, overlooking that he was an expert on the Middle East, a fluent speaker of Arabic, and an officer who had served the 'old' Agency with distinction.

But George hadn't come to Caracas because of work or to visit us. He was on a mission for his Ukrainian aunt in Chicago.

George's cousin in Caracas, a recent widower, had fallen ill and needed help. I've a distinct memory of the night George returned to our residence from his cousin's apartment. He called upstairs to Michelle and Bonnie, high school students and close in age to George's two daughters. In the foyer that evening, George stood beside two large suitcases.

Mike and I, and our daughters wondered what was inside.

Furs, lots of them, from George's cousin's deceased wife. And laughing as only George laughed, he said, "Model them, girls!" Who could ignore a request from George? Not my daughters. They pranced about, making exits from the garden room, returning each time in a different fur coat or stole, once with the beady-eyed head of a fox.

I asked George where his cousin's wife could have worn furs. Not in Caracas surely, with its mild climate. We had no air conditioning and left the windows open year-round. George asked if I remembered Papa Doc, the dictator of Haiti. Did I know that his wife had a wardrobe of furs? Which was why Papa Doc had ordered that a huge, refrigerated room had to be built, so his wife could entertain her friends, with all of them wearing furs?

"And your point in telling me this, George?"

"There's something I need you to do for me."

Ah, I thought, the request moment!

It turned out that George needed my help with transporting a large collection of jewelry, which a Venezuelan-Ukrainian woman was keeping for his cousin. The woman was away and would not return before he left Caracas, George said, adding that his diplomatic passport days were numbered. "Not yours." George meant that when I traveled from Venezuela to Miami, as I did on occasion, my possessions would not be searched.

In January 1993, George sent Jalila to Caracas on behalf of his Ukrainian relatives. Since George's visit, the dying cousin had moved to Chicago to live with the aunt. But the jewelry was still in Venezuela. Unfortunately, recent events had more than shaken Jalila. She and George had lost their Miami home in Hurricane Andrew. The same week of Andrew's destruction, Jalila learned a sister in Tunis had died suddenly. A few days after Andrew, a driver rear-ended Jalila's car and left her with a lingering neck injury. Now, more than a year later, she had not fully recovered.

The night before Jalila left Caracas to return to Miami, she dined at the Ukrainian woman's house, returning that evening to our residence with some of the jewelry, which I did not see until the following morning. Jalila came down the stairs to the garden room, looking elegant as always: long dark hair, soulful eyes, in attire respectful of her Islamic faith. Only now she was draped in gold: earrings, necklaces, bracelets, even anklets. She stopped in front of the sofa where I sat and shook her arms, which set the bracelets jangling. "This is how whores in Tunis call attention." She shook the bracelets again. "Look at me! A Tunisian Whore! I will kill George."

"Leave the jewelry here," I said. "I'll get it to Miami in two months."

"Leave it here? There is already too much for you. You think I wear all the jewelry? More is in my purse," she said, adding that the Ukrainian woman would bring the expensive jewelry to me. "George knows no one in the airport will search you."

"Maybe we should both kill George," I teased. Only then did Jalila laugh. Yet I knew her emotional and physical pain from the preceding year remained layered, like the gold jewelry she reluctantly wore that morning.

Weeks later Mrs. L. stood at the gate to our residence in silvery high heels and tight pants. I invited her and her daughter to the garden room where there was a large accessible table for the jewelry. She spoke a slower Spanish than the typical Venezuelan. For this I was grateful. The adolescent daughter had blond hair like the mother, and her face betrayed no impatience when her mother handed her a two-page list and a pen. Then Mrs. L. began removing pieces of wrapped jewelry from an old canvas bank bag with faded black lettering. The first item, wrapped in white tissue paper, was a gigantic amethyst ring, surrounded by green stones, the gem at the center as large as my big toe. Mrs. L. explained that her Ukrainian friend and his deceased wife were not rich, adding an odd description of the wife: "*La coqueta era muy corta.*" I heard *short* and thought of the furs. A full-length mink had not reached my younger daughter Bonnie's knees.

Other rings appeared, each enormous like the gaudy amethyst. The daughter checked more items off the inventory. I offered refreshments, which Mrs. L. refused. I sensed that for her only the telling of the tale was important. *La coqueta* had been childless, a *closed* woman, and even at the end had not sounded a cry for help until too late. Mrs. L. described the tiny woman gasping for breath, being rushed to the hospital, dying there the following day.

I asked about the woman's husband, George's cousin.

Mrs. L's unlined face did not show the agitation I heard in her voice when she told me her friend had been bed-ridden in the couple's apartment and saddled with a medical bill he could not afford. Slowly through a haze of translation, I grasped the subtext. The husband had been Mrs. L's idol, a close friend of her parents, a man she had adored from early childhood in a small Ukrainian-Venezuelan community of exiles. Now I understood why she had been entrusted with the jewelry. She told me that her ill Ukrainian friend had left Caracas in 1992, shortly after George's visit, and gone to live with his aunt in Chicago. I already knew this but said nothing.

Mrs. L. started to remove the tissue paper from another large ring but stopped midway. She wanted me to understand that before *la coqueta's* death, the aunt had shown no concern for her nephew in Caracas, had not visited him, yet now expressed interest in the sale of the apartment. With the half-full bag of jewelry on the table and the tissue paper still in her hand, she told me that after *la coqueta's* death, the aunt had written and asked Mrs. L. if she would take care of the nephew. "*Que audacia!*" she said. I nodded in agreement. Yes, it seemed an *audacious* request.

The daughter listened and never interrupted. I thought of my impatient daughter Bonnie, who would have sworn in Venezuelan Spanish. *Conchale, Mamacita. I've heard the story a hundred times.* I pause, reconsider my words. For George, Bonnie would have listened.

That afternoon in Caracas, Mrs. L.'s story *had* to be told.

And like the daughter, I listened. After *la coqueta* died, George's ill cousin had hidden his wife's jewelry inside an empty toilet-tank and forbidden the maid to enter the bathroom located close to his bed. Domestic help had ransacked the apartment of valuable objects, an unscrupulous lawyer stole an expensive silver tea set. But Mrs. L. and her husband had saved the jewelry from thieving hands. She pointed to what lay on the glass coffee table, said the jewelry was expensive when bought, now worth so much less. The silver goblets, the ones that hadn't been stolen, fetched a mere 40 thousand *bolivares*, fewer than two hundred dollars.

The afternoon waned, more than an hour had passed. Half of the items had not been unwrapped. Again, I offered refreshments. No, they *really* had to be going. I knew, however, that Mrs. L. would not leave until she finished her story. She stopped opening jewelry and spread several photographs on the table. One showed *la coqueta* with a Catholic cardinal at the Vatican. The tiny woman had been devoted to the church. And wherever she went, if only to shop in Caracas, she wore large jewels and furs, her blond hair perfectly styled. I remember staring at the ragged-edged photographs on the table that day. In several photos the husband (George's cousin) held a cigarette in one of those holders I associate with aristocrats. I'd recently seen *Schindler's List* and George's cousin was Liam Neeson's double: tall, wavy hair, a romantic gaze, elegant attire—the kind of man a young girl would idolize and love.

The sky was darkening. I asked if they would like coffee, perhaps a glass of wine. No, they were leaving. Then came the final unwrapping of the jewelry, nothing of special value—gold and silver crosses, some with semi-precious stones. The daughter handed me the inventory with each item checked off, and I signed my name on both pages. Then a hesitant departure, kisses on both cheeks, effusive thanks that I was willing to transport the jewelry to George, and to free Mrs. L. of a burden she had carried for too long. I recall suppressing a smile. I knew from what Jalila had told me, that Mrs. L. had kept several pieces of expensive jewelry, including a valuable emerald, which she claimed was a ring George's cousin had given her after *la coqueta's* death. This was not reiterated in the garden room where throughout the afternoon I kept noticing the large emerald ring on her finger as she unwound tissue paper from the jewelry.

That late afternoon the mother and daughter walked through the gate on *Calle San Pedro*, and I shut it behind them. To this day I retain the sound of that peculiar clang from the heavy, metal grates that protected each door and window to our embassy residence. The sound always reminded me that like a prisoner, I was again behind gates and locked grates in Caracas, where it was perilous to expose jewelry, and where the mild temperature meant it was never cold enough to wear a fur.

I waited until Mrs. L's car left, then returned to the garden room to gather the things on the table. Among the photographs was a Venezuelan identity card. I picked it up, studied the *la coqueta's* small photo, felt the loneliness of a life reduced to a national identity card—on a glass table in a stranger's home?

What I recall as distinctly as that afternoon was the one after it.

I, along with other embassy wives, attended a luncheon at

172

the ambassador's residence high on a hill above Caracas. We ate at two large circular tables on the patio. At one point, finding the conversation tedious, I noticed the *charger* beneath my plate. In memory I see a swirl of colors in the china, and beneath that plate a larger one in cobalt blue. I remember thinking that my husband, the Defense Attaché, ought to be using chargers with our *official* white and gold china. But the Air Force did not provide the plates, which meant we would have had to buy them, and I wanted to begin shedding material objects.

As promised, I later delivered the jewelry to Miami. After we'd unpacked all of it in George and Jalila's house, rebuilt after Hurricane Andrew, George asked if there was anything I would like. I pointed to a dainty garnet necklace with matching earrings, the only subtle piece in *la coqueta's* collection. "Then it's yours," George said, adding that he would speak to his aunt in Chicago about giving me the set. Maybe the aunt declined, or George forgot. No matter, as I had no real connection to the jewelry and wanted fewer possessions in life. Yet when I left Miami, George insisted that I take with me a piece of folk art from his Ukrainian homeland. The plate was the size of the *charger* I'd just seen in Caracas, but this plate was made of honey-colored wood, with a mosaic of inlaid pearl and tiny stones. Wanting to have something emblematic of George and his life, I accepted the gift.

In 1996, George and Jalila stopped for an overnight at our townhouse near D.C. They were on their way to New York where George's brother was hospitalized and not expected to live. Over breakfast George commented on the Ukrainian plate on a nearby wall. Until that morning I hadn't known the plate's twin had been badly damaged during Hurricane Andrew when the roof blew off the house. The plate was found among the ruin of their things collected from decades of postings in the Middle East and Southeast Asia. The news shocked me, that George had given me the surviving plate.

"You must take this one with you," I said.

He set his penetrating blue eyes on me. "No. Keep it in memory of me."

I think now of the plate's journey from Ukraine to the West, and of George—one of life's truly memorable characters, a man we all loved. In 2010, he fought lung cancer, appeared to have won an arduous match against it, then died suddenly one morning in Jalila's arms from a heart attack. In the months following George's death and for several more years, whenever Jalila and I spoke by phone, she recounted the terrible loss of the man she had loved to the depth of her soul. Then more shadows of calamity and sadder news. Jalila had stopped chemo after her surgery for brain cancer and returned to Tunisia. She died there in January 2015, buried in her homeland alongside her father, mother, and siblings.

Yet Jalila's illness and death reconnected me with her daughter.

One spring day, looking at the plate on the wall above the staircase, I thought of George's exile from his homeland. It was at that moment I knew the Ukrainian plate belonged to his daughter, not to me. And now the mystical-patterned plate hangs on his daughter's wall in Florida, where one day her young children will hear the story of their grandfather and learn how far the Ukrainian plate traveled to be with them.

To part with the jewelry, Mrs. L. had to tell her story.

I needed to write about George to let go of an object that had not belonged to me. As an aging woman, I struggle terribly with what the Germans call *Die Sehnsucht*, a painful longing for that, which is no more. And yet, despite recognizing this truth, I yearn to again run wildly beneath the Malaysian sun, trying to win the tennis match quickly and keep George from having a heart attack.

What can I, who am old, say to Mr. Death?

Only that the blue-eyed boy and his soulful wife live in memory through these written words.

The Last Point

I began *Tennis Talk of a Nobody* with a quote from my living literary hero, Robert Coles. I end with a quote from my deceased literary hero, Anton Chekhov. Both men used the word, fate. In a letter, Chekhov wrote: "Yes, they will forget us. Such is our *fate*, there is no hope for it. What seems to us serious, significant, very important, will one day be forgotten or will seem unimportant. And it is curious that we cannot tell what exactly will be considered great and important, and what will seem petty and ridiculous...'

Yes, dear Anton, admittedly this is true. But in tennis the joy I have found is in movement, an essential for a healthy life, and neither ridiculous nor petty. And for a player like me, tennis has been for seventy years a complex and trans-figurative experience. What changed with age was the sport's meaning. It became not about winning and losing, not the score of a match, and not the ranking on a ladder or in public record. Tennis became a durable pleasure in life.

The joy of this sport is in running and swinging a racquet. In tennis I experience a conjunction of recurrence and newness. I love the range of shot-making on a court of varied surface with set dimensions. Always there is the promise of combining strokes and creating a desired effect. I especially find delight in hitting a flat stroke that barely crosses the net, or of sending a lob into the air that lands on the backline, and of daring a dropshot that dies a foot from the net. An even greater pleasure has been with me since my youthful days of competitive play. I keep slicing crosscourt backhands, then suddenly drive one smack down the line. Unfortunately, since knee replacement and months away from the courts, my serve took a leave of absence. I've yet to find it. But occasionally I have a service ace on the mid-court line or drop a disguised slice just over the net. Now what I lack in power, I try to achieve through stealth. And now there is a shot I never tried with a wood racquet: a swinging volley from 'no man's land'.

Oh, so much joy in playing tennis. In moving back and forth on the baseline, up and over at the net, springing here, stretching there, mindful always of maintaining focused eyes and dancing feet. Best of all is this. Tennis makes a promise. The game is not over until the last point. I like to think mine will come as I run for a wide forehand and hit a winner from the alley. What a way to say good-bye!

I end with three words. Thank you, Tennis. You gave me a durable pleasure and were the conveyer of life's two C's: Chance and Circumstance. Yet I must add the third and most important C of all. Connection... in the great weave of life itself.